THE

LANDING

OF THE

PILGRIMS

Written and Illustrated by

JAMES DAUGHERTY

RANDOM HOUSE · NEW YORK

This title was originally catalogued by the Library of Congress as follows:

Daugherty, James Henry, 1889–
  The landing of the Pilgrims; written and illustrated by
James Daugherty. New York, Random House [1950]

    vi, 186 p. col. illus. 22 cm. (Landmark books [2])

    1. Massachusetts—Hist.—Colonial period (New Plymouth)—Fic-
tion.   1. Title.

PZ7.D2625Lan   50—10542

Lib. Ed.: ISBN: 0-394-90302-1

Contents

PART THREE:

New England Adventure 1621-1623

PART ONE

Not As Other Men
1607-1620

The Boy and the Postmaster
(1607)

THE BLAST OF THE COURIER'S HORN SOUNDED gaily across the fields. The post riders were nearing the town of Scrooby on the great North Road from London. The dogs barked, and children ran out shouting. A few villagers hurried toward the big house called the Manor. All were eager to see the post riders change horses in the Manor courtyard.

Young Will Bradford heard the noise and broke into a run. If he hurried now he would be just in time to see the riders gallop in. As Will came panting into the courtyard, the stable boys led out the two fresh horses. The animals were saddled and all ready to be mounted by the post riders who were about to arrive.

In a few moments the horn sounded again. The two riders came pounding over the drawbridge on their lathering horses, and through the gate to the Manor courtyard.

The post rider in his high boots and scarlet coat leaped from his horse and quickly unstrapped the two leather mail bags.

At that moment, William Brewster, the Postmaster of Scrooby, came down the stone steps of the Manor to receive the mail. While Brewster entered the contents of the post bags in his books of registry, the post rider and his bugler were guzzling their dinner of cold mutton and beer. In fifteen minutes they must be riding their fresh mounts north on the road toward York.

Having finished the meal, they swung into the saddle and were off. The gay notes of the postman's horn faded sweetly into the distance. The village again settled back into the drowsy dullness of a long afternoon.

Not so William Brewster, who, with his many

duties, found little time for idleness. Brewster, as Postmaster at Scrooby, was the great man of the countryside. He was Steward of the Manor and collected the rents from the tenants of the wide domain of the Archbishop of York. He was the administrator of law and justice for the district. A man of learning, Brewster had attended Cambridge in his youth where he had studied Greek and Latin.

Later, in the service of Queen Elizabeth, he had accompanied one of her ambassadors on an important mission to the Low Countries. He had seen the great world, yet he had come back to this remote corner of England to be Postmaster at Scrooby where his father had held the same office.

Although Brewster had moved among the great ones of his day, he was neither proud nor vain. He was respected by his neighbors for his wisdom and godliness. When a neighbor was sick or in trouble and needed the help of a friend, he knew that he could find it at the hands of the Postmaster of Scrooby Manor.

No one had felt the warmth of Master Brewster's kindness more than young Will Bradford, who looked to him almost as a father. When the boy had been left an orphan and was long ill, Master Brewster had often traveled the two miles from Scrooby to Austerfield, to visit him and bring presents. As young Will slowly recovered, his friend had helped him in his studies and had given him a copy of the Bible printed in English at Geneva. This Geneva Bible was still a new and rare book in that part of England. Will spent happy hours absorbed in its wondrous pages. He and the Postmaster often talked together of its beauty and meaning. In hours of loneliness and pain the Book had brought the boy a marvelous comfort and peace.

Later when Will had visited Master Brewster at the Manor, he had heard him tell brave tales of the great world of London and of the brilliant court of Queen Bess. The lad thrilled to hear the story of how, in 1588, the year before he was born, the terrible Armada of King Philip, with all the might of Spain, had sailed against England; and of how Sir Francis Drake and his fearless sea dogs had sallied forth against the great array.

Will felt as if he himself had been upon the English decks in all the flame and thunder of the fierce encounter. In the night, Drake had loosed the terrible fire ships blazing among the Spanish fleet. Cutting their cables, the Spaniards had put to sea, and a great wind had blown them toward the coast of Holland. There the English gunners hammered the enemy to pieces as the great hulks of Spain's proudest ships went up in smoke and flame.

In his imagination young Will pictured himself as a sea captain capturing treasure ships on the Spanish Main. "When I become a man," he thought, "I shall sail a ship across the wide ocean sea and go adventuring among the savages in wild America."

Now he was in his teens and had never even seen the sea, although the coast was but fifty miles from where he lived. Perhaps he never would see it, for his uncles planned, very sensibly, that he should be a farmer and cultivate the goodly lands his father had left him.

How Will Made a Great Decision

For some time Will had heard people talking about a preacher at Babsworth who spoke of the Bible with great power. Because Will read and loved the Bible, he decided to hear this man. It was a twenty-mile walk to Babsworth and back, but Mr. Richard Clyfton's preaching was worth all the trouble.

After that first trip, Will often walked there to hear Mr. Clyfton read and expound the Scriptures. The boy seldom missed a Sunday, even if his uncles did not approve of reformist preachers.

Later Master Brewster asked Clyfton to preach on Sundays in the great hall at Scrooby Manor. The Postmaster invited friends and neighbors to come and hear Mr. Clyfton preach. It was not long before many people began attending regularly every Sunday. Folks said Mr. Clyfton's discourses woke them up to understand the Scriptures. They came away from these meetings happy and comforted. They began to read and to study their Bible and to try and practice its teaching in their daily lives. Master Brewster explained that in this simple way the first Christian churches began in ancient times.

Within a year the congregation at Scrooby Manor decided to form a church of their own. It was to be entirely separate from the State Church of England, and would have no bishops or ceremonies. For this reason they would call themselves Separatists. They would also separate themselves from the Puritans, who wanted to reform the Church of England but not to separate from it.

How Persecution Came Upon the Separatists at Scrooby

When Young William Bradford announced to his friends that he would leave the church in which he had been baptized and join the Separatists, people were shocked. His uncles pointed out that he would certainly come to a bad end. Already men had been hung for holding onto such ideas. Friends and relatives argued, pleaded, threatened, warned, but to no purpose. He calmly replied:

"To keep a good conscience and walk in such Way as God had prescribed in his Word, is a thing which I must prefer before you all, and above life itself. Wherefore, since it is for a good Cause that I am likely to suffer the disasters which you lay before me, you have no cause to be either angry with me, or sorry for me. Yea, I am not only willing to part with everything that is dear to me in this world for this Cause but I am thankful that God hath given me heart so to do: and will accept me so to suffer for him."

Plainly the boy was mad.

Spies and informers began to watch the homes and to dog the steps of the members of the Separatist Church. The congregation now met secretly at different times and places. One member was arrested and tried by the Archbishop's Court at York. He was imprisoned and then released. Five more members, including Master Brewster, were summoned to appear before the court. William did not need to seek abroad for adventure. Danger waited for him around every corner.

It was becoming clear to the Separatists that there could be no freedom for their religion in England. They must shake off the dust of the corrupt land and seek for freedom of pure religion elsewhere. Already one congregation of Protestants had gone to Holland. Master Brewster said that it was a land where there was perfect freedom of religion, as he had seen in his travels.

The Scrooby Separatists decided to go to Holland, as Master Brewster had advised. However, they knew that no one could leave England or take out goods and money without permission from the government. This meant that they would have to flee secretly like criminals. It was a hard and cruel thing to leave one's home and country in this way and seek a living in a strange land.

Mr. Brewster and the few who owned land sold their possessions. Secretly, arrangements were made with a Dutch ship captain to meet them at the coast and carry them to Amsterdam. There would be no farewells to their neighbors, for their leaving must be kept as secret as possible.

The women with their few belongings would float in a barge to the coast. The men would walk across country a distance of fifty miles to the meeting place.

Departure
(1608)

The first streak of dawn was breaking on the horizon. A chill east wind blew across the marshes near the coast. The women in the barge were seasick from the rough voyage they had made to the meeting place. They were worried, too, for neither the Dutch ship nor their own men had arrived.

Their craft had put into an inlet to be sheltered from the rough sea, but now the tide was going out. Soon the water in the inlet was so low that the barge was left stranded on a sand bar. Not until noon would the tide rise enough to float them off.

As the sky brightened, the women heard familiar voices calling. Their men had come at last! The walk across country to the coast had taken them two days.

It was light now, and the men from Scrooby could see the Dutch ship off shore. They could start boarding the ship at once, but the women and children would have to wait until noon when the rising tide would free their barge.

The Dutch ship's boat came ashore to take on passengers. She returned to the ship with the first boatload of men. Among them was William Bradford, now a young man of nineteen years.

Suddenly those still on shore heard shouting and excited cries from the ship. As they looked out to sea, she began making sail. Now she was hauling up her anchors! Slowly the huge sails filled. The ship was putting out to sea.

On shore women screamed and men shouted wildly. They had been abandoned—left on shore while the rest of their party sailed off to Holland. It was a heartbreaking end to their hopes and plans.

Those who were left behind could now see a band of men coming toward them across the marshes, with glint of light on armor and pikes.

It had been foolish to suppose that a hundred people marching across country for fifty miles would not be seen by the spies and informers. There was time for most of the men ashore to escape. A few at Brewster's command remained with the women.

The King's soldiers marched the unhappy group of deserted women and children back to the nearest town. The magistrates were at a loss what to do with them. There was no charge that could really be brought against them, as they had only followed their husbands. To send them to jail would merely arouse sympathy for the Separatists. They could not be sent home because all their homes had been sold. As friends were found who would give them temporary shelter, they were released.

The whole countryside had heard of their misfortune and of their courage in the face of persecution. It all increased the people's sympathy for the Separatists.

In the meantime the unhappy Englishmen aboard the Dutch ship were bound for Holland. They had neither money nor clothes, and they were miserably anxious for their wives and children left behind. They knew that the captain had had to hasten his departure because of the oncoming soldiers, but this knowledge was of small comfort to them.

Bradford was at last on the ocean, but it was very different from his boyhood dreams. For a week the ship ran before a lashing gale. At times it seemed that she would surely sink. When the weather cleared they had been blown to the coasts of Norway.

When they finally arrived at Amsterdam, they found that the ship had been given up as lost. People said that their survival was a miracle. On landing, William Bradford was promptly arrested. The agent of the King of England had told the Dutch government that Bradford was an escaped criminal. In a few days he was able to prove that he was a religious refugee. Immediately he was freed, and welcomed by the English Protestant exiles who were then living in Holland.

By degrees the rest of the refugees arrived in small groups from England until the entire Scrooby congregation was again united in this foreign land. The last to come was Master Brewster. He had been jailed, and when released, had aided the remaining families to find passage to Holland.

For the first time these English country folk

were in a big city. They gawked with wide eyes at the well-dressed crowds, the soldiers posted at the gates and walls, the crowded docks, the overflowing markets and the rows of handsome dwellings.

Best of all, they had at last found freedom to worship God as they chose. They openly attended church on Sundays without fear of spies. Soon they joined the reformed English Church already established in Amsterdam and set about finding ways to make their living in the trades and industries of the busy city.

Master Brewster now became unhappily aware of a new threat to their religion—a threat that was even more dangerous than persecution. It did not take the one-time Postmaster of Scrooby long to discover that the Amsterdam Church was divided with controversy and personal quarrels. There were accusations, slander, and backbiting everywhere among the members. This, Master Brewster thought, was not living the Christian teachings of the Bible.

To escape becoming entangled in these mean quarrels and feuds, the Scrooby Separatists decided to move on again. As pilgrims, they would journey to the city of Leyden. This city attracted them because it was famous throughout the world for its University and its brave resistance to the Spaniards.

When the Scrooby folk were ready to make this second move, they had a grave disappointment. At the last moment their pastor, Richard Clyfton, refused to leave the Amsterdam Church. They chose their beloved teacher, John Robinson, to be their pastor in his stead.

Leyden Years
(1608-1620)

They made the pleasant twenty-four-mile journey from Amsterdam to Leyden by canal boat, passing through level land that stretched like a garden to the horizon. In the distance, church spires rose and everywhere were windmills with their great sails turning in the fresh sea wind.

At the city gate of Leyden, the guard examined their papers. Then the newcomers passed under the deep arch into the ancient city which was to be their home.

Leyden was called, by the many who loved her, the fairest and most civilized city in the world. It was a prosperous city too, and there the strangers soon found employment as weavers, hatters, printers, carpenters and craftsmen in a dozen other trades. Their pay was usually small and their hours long, but in time they were able to buy a large house for their pastor in Bell Alley near the cathedral. A plot of land was purchased, and houses for the church members were built around a quiet court.

This colony became a peaceful bit of England planted in a corner of the friendly Dutch city. Here they welcomed other English refugees to the freedom and peace of their new home, and the congregation grew in numbers and strengthened in faith. Their wise and loving Pastor John Robinson became a father unto them, and his congregation grew in grace and mutual love.

Elder Brewster taught English in the University. It was a popular course, and he was able to provide comfortably for his wife and three children.

Young Bradford became a maker of corduroy. As he prospered, he courted and married Dorothy May of Wisbeach, England. Their wedding took place at the Leyden city hall. According to the Separatists, marriage was performed by the magistrates and not by the Church.

Soon Bradford could speak Dutch like a Hollander, and French like—well, he could manage it somehow. He became a good Latin and Greek scholar and loved to study Hebrew with the hope that someday he would be able to read the Bible in the original tongue. He made many friends among the hospitable Hollanders and became a Dutch citizen.

On peaceful Sundays, Bradford and the other English exiles walked along brick-paved streets under the delicate linden trees that bordered the quiet Razenbutts Canal. They marveled at the great cathedral and the handsome Stadhouse. Prosperous Dutch burghers and their wives strolled by dressed in silks and fine linen.

Sometimes, through open doorways, the Scrooby folk caught glimpses of richly furnished rooms where a silk-clad girl strummed a mandolin. On the floors were rich Turkey carpets and the walls were decorated with hangings, engraved maps, or pictures of calm merchants in sober black. Dutch kitchens gleamed with pots and pans of polished copper, and tables were piled with fruit from the market stalls along the Rhine.

One Sunday afternoon Bradford stopped before

a book-shop window to study curious prints picturing the barbarous customs of the savages of Florida and Virginia. The pictures were in a book of Voyages newly published by the engraver Theodore de Bry.

Every one of the exiles found something to love in this friendly city, and to the English boys and girls it soon became home. They learned to sing and dance at the rollicking Dutch Kermess, or harvest festival. In winter they strapped on their curved wooden skates and flew over the ice outside the city walls.

The Press

No one knew better than the scholarly Brewster the power of the printed word to influence the minds of men. He had long dreamed of a printing press to spread the true religion as the Separatists saw it. In England presses must be licensed and all printing was censored by the King and the Bishop.

When Elder Brewster became used to the free air of Leyden, he realized that this was the place to start his press. For it, his friend Mr. Brewer provided the money. Soon Separatists' tracts and pamphlets from Brewster's press were being smuggled into England and secretly circulated.

King James was especially annoyed at two pamphlets which denounced the Perth Assembly. (At this Assembly of Scotch clergymen, the King had attempted to compel them to conform to the Church of England and its practices.) It was known that these books were being smuggled in from Holland, and the King's spies were searching Amsterdam and Leyden for the secret press, and particularly for the person of Mr. Brewster.

The will of King James was almost as powerful in Holland as in England, for English troops had long fought in the Lowlands (for a price), aiding the Dutch against the Spanish. Because of this, it was not long before the authorities at Leyden quietly closed down Mr. Brewster's printing press. But Mr. Brewster himself was nowhere to be found. The truth is that he was on a secret mission to his old home in Scrooby.

There he was discussing with his old friend and landlord, Sir Edwin Sandys, the Separatists' plans to seek a new home.

Brewster realized that no time must be lost in

seeking another place to live, for Holland's twelve-year peace treaty with Spain was drawing to a close. The English exiles at Leyden would soon find themselves in a country torn by war.

Furthermore, new problems had appeared. The King's spies were again hounding the Separatist leaders. Their children were growing up barely remembering old England. Some had married Dutch girls and boys. Others had gone to sea on the Dutch ships that sailed to the distant East Indies. Their sons joined the Dutch army as musketeers and were marching in cutlass and helmet through the streets of Leyden to the sound of drum and trumpet, prepared for war.

Few Hollanders had been converted to the Separatist Church. On the contrary, there was a real danger of the whole English colony becoming slowly absorbed into Dutch life. The Separatists treasured and valued their mother tongue and English nationality second only to their religion. It was becoming plain that the only place where they could still remain Englishmen and keep their freedom of worship was across the ocean in the wilderness of America.

William and Dorothy Bradford spoke of these

things as they sometimes walked on the ancient walls of Leyden in the quiet evening.

"Why can we not stay among our friends in this peaceful city?" urged Dorothy. "Some time things will change, perhaps, and we can go back to the old home in England. Why should we be forever moving on?"

"Things will grow worse in England, not better," William replied. "As the King forces his will upon the people, there will be no more freedom in England.

"America is the promised land," he went on. "There we can found a new state where freedom-loving men may come. The Word of God will be a shining light to all the world. We shall build the New Jerusalem, and the kings of the earth shall bring their glory and honor into it."

For the moment Dorothy was caught in the fervor of his words. She knew that he would go and that she would go with him. Yet in her dreams, England would always be calling her back to a peaceful garden and a quiet street and the spring wind blowing over the flower-strewn meadows.

William and Dorothy were not the only people who were divided on the question of going to

25

America. Never had there been such discussion and argument since the English had come to Leyden. Everyone took sides in the matter of leaving Holland for America. Those who were against it spoke of the dangers and great length of the sea voyage, the sufferings from famine and want in the savage wilderness. When it came to the Indian perils, they really let their imaginations go and described in detail what it felt like to be skinned, broiled, and eaten by the savages. Besides all these unpleasantnesses, it would cost a great deal more than any of them could afford.

Bradford replied for those who were determined to go:

"All great and honorable actions are accompanied with great difficulties; and must be both enterprised and overcome with answerable courages. It was granted the dangers were great, but not desperate; the difficulties were many, but not invincible. For though there were many of them likely, yet they were not certain. It might be that sundry of the things feared might never befall; others, by provident care and the use of good means, might in a great measure be prevented; and all of them, through the help of

God, *by fortitude and patience, might either be borne or overcome.*"

The words glowed with faith and vision and an unbeatable courage to build a brave free world. As always before great decisions, there was a day of prayer by the congregation. When the vote was taken according to their democratic custom, the majority were for going to the New World, for moving on, for the great Adventure.

There were now many more decisions to be made and much to be done. Just where they should go and how many of them should go, were serious questions. While the King's agents were looking for him in Holland, Mr. Brewster was in England with his friend Sir Edwin Sandys, urging him to persuade the King to grant them freedom of religion in America.

Those in Leyden who were going to the New World sold their property. Funds were raised. A ship named the "Speedwell" was ordered to be fitted and provisioned. Then it was to await their embarkation at Delfthaven.

Among the friends of those about to sail in the "Speedwell" was a Mr. Weston, a British merchant of enterprise. When he had heard of their intentions to go to America, he had come to Leyden. Mr. Weston offered to form a company of merchant adventurers, in which all would have shares. The Adventurers, as the merchants were called, would provide what funds were needed for the trip and would send the colony supplies.

In return, the plantation in America would ship back fish, furs, and any other products of the new world that would be of profit to the company. At the end of seven years the profits would be divided among the shareholders. After much discussion of details, a seven-year contract with terms agreeable to all was signed by the agents of both parties in London.

Already the Dutch had offered the Leyden Separatists free transportation to the Island of Manhattan on the Hudson River and a cow for each family, if they would settle there. But they wanted to remain British subjects wherever they might go, and so refused.

Delfthaven Farewell
(August, 1620)

The wind was fair and the tide was at the flood. On the main deck of the "Speedwell" the Separatists and their friends knelt with streaming eyes. Mr. Robinson was not going on this trip, but he led them in prayer. Tenderly they gazed into the faces of their loved ones who were remaining behind. They might never meet again. "Good-bye, good-bye, dear hearts, until we meet again."

The last friend had gone ashore. The mate

shouted his orders. The hawsers were cast off. Slowly the ship moved from the dock, a few feet, a few yards. She was under way. Along the ship's rail the travelers stood waving farewell. The figures on the quay diminished and blurred. Sharply a volley of musket and a salute of three guns rang out from the ship. Soon she was out on the broad waters of the River Maas. Shortly they had passed the Hook, westward bound for England. In four days they would reach Southampton.

From the "Speedwell's" deck, Dorothy and William Bradford watched the low shore line dropping behind. Memory-pictures of the good years crowded their thoughts. Warm-hearted, liberal Holland, hospitable Leyden, the peaceful homes in Bell Alley, their genial Dutch neighbors so courteous and understanding through twelve pleasant years, all blended in a colored mist of affectionate remembrance.

Steadily the ship drove westward before the wind, and those aboard turned their thoughts toward the future. All told, there were thirty-three of the Leyden congregation who had volunteered for the great adventure. If they succeeded, Mr. Robinson and the others would join them in the new land. Among the pilgrims were the stoutest pillars of their church, Brewster, Bradford, Winslow and Carver, Allerton and their surgeon, Samuel Fuller. Come good or ill, these could be counted as steadfast rock.

Already their situation was complicated with difficulties and delays. At Southampton they found their agent Cushman waiting. He had agreed with the merchants' demands to make certain changes in their contract.

These new conditions the Separatists would not accept. They would not agree to terms that bound them to what was practically slavery for seven years. Afterward they would have to divide their lands and properties with the merchants. They had agreed to work four days every week for the company. Cushman now said the merchants insisted that they must work six days a week for the company for a seven-year period. For this the merchants were to furnish them with sufficient supplies of food, clothing, tools, and trading goods for Indian barter

Aboard the "Mayflower"

(August, 1620)

At Southampton the one-hundred-and-eighty-ton ship "Mayflower" rode at anchor. Provisioned and ready to sail, she had been awaiting the arrival of the "Speedwell" for a week. Awaiting it too was Mr. Weston, who had come down from London to urge and argue that the "Speedwell's" passengers sign the new terms with the merchant adventurers. The Pilgrims again firmly refused. Mr. Weston left them in a rage, refusing to make any more payments. There was a port charge of one hundred pounds still to be paid. They sold their surplus firkins of butter to raise this amount.

Sixty-seven passengers from England were now added to the thirty-three from Leyden. Only nine of the company were over forty years of age. Winslow was twenty-five, Bradford thirty-one, and Standish thirty-six. There were thirty-nine boys and girls under age.

Captain John Smith of Virginia fame had sent a message to them offering his services. They had already engaged Captain Miles Standish, a veteran of the Lowland wars, to be their military commander.

Captain Standish was aboard ship now. He was a short, broad man with his long rapier hung at his side. He was seeing that the muskets and ammunition were properly stored in the ship's gun room.

Among the Londoners, Stephen Hopkins was helping stow the baggage between decks. His wife and two children were chatting with the Mullins family.

Young Priscilla Mullins and her little brother were talking to a young London cooper named John Alden. "Is it really true that the savages broil and eat English children?" asked Priscilla.

Like the rest of the Pilgrims, John had heard fearful tales about the Indians. He didn't know if they were true or not, but he spoke bravely and did his best to comfort Priscilla.

A rough-looking Mr. Billington and his wife were warning their two mischievous boys not to touch the muskets.

When all was ready for the departure, Mr. Brewster called the congregation together and read them Mr. Robinson's letter of counsel and farewell. Then with full hearts and brave hopes they knelt and prayed:

"They that go down to the sea in ships, and that do business in great waters, those see the works of the Lord, and His wonders in the deep. He maketh the storm calm, so that the waves thereof are still. Then are they glad because they be quiet; so He bringeth them to their desired haven. Oh, that men would praise the Lord for His goodness, and for His wonderful works to the children of men!"

As the "Speedwell" and the "Mayflower" moved seaward, Bradford felt deeply relieved. He had watched anxiously each day. He feared lest the King's soldiers and the Bishops' spies might at the last minute appear and drag them off to jail.

As the shores of England dropped under the horizon, he remembered his boyhood dreams of sea voyaging. Now he was outward bound for freedom. The "Mayflower" was nosing westward into the green Atlantic.

Suddenly the mate called to Captain Jones, who was talking with Elder Brewster at the half-deck rail. "The lookout reports the 'Speedwell' has put out distress signals, Sir," the mate warned.

At once the "Mayflower" shortened sail and the "Speedwell" overtook her. Master Reynolds of the "Speedwell" reported that his ship was leaking badly. There was nothing to do but make for the nearest port. At Dartmouth, the "Speedwell" was overhauled from stem to stern and all leaks mended.

Again a fair wind filled their sails. The two ships steadily drove westward for some three hundred miles. Again the "Speedwell" signaled distress. Master Reynolds reported that she was taking on water so fast that the pumps could barely keep her afloat. The two ships put back to Plymouth. No leaks were found in the "Speedwell" but the captains concluded she was overmasted and unseaworthy.

It was suspected that Reynolds had done this deliberately because he and the crew did not really want to go to America. Afterward, when she was properly fitted, the "Speedwell" proved to be a good ship. Again the harassed Pilgrims changed their plans. They would send the "Speedwell" back to London and go on in the "Mayflower" with what passengers and supplies they could take on from the smaller ship.

Mr. Cushman, the agent, and some twenty of the most disheartened of the passengers, returned to London. Precious time and money had been lost. Provisions had been used up, and it seemed that every possible trouble and discouragement had arisen to block their way. September had arrived. Worst of all, winter would be upon them by the time they reached the shores of Virginia.

Dorothy Bradford was discouraged to the point of tears, but William put his arm around her shoulder and said, quoting Master Brewster's words:

"It is not with us as with other men whom small things can discourage, or small discontentments cause to wish themselves at home again."

These would be good words for him to recall in the dark times that might come. They had a comforting sound for men plowing westward through perilous seas toward unknown shores. The phrases had a rhythm for swinging axes and feet marching through mountain passes and across thirsty plains in unknown lands. The words had a lift of heart for idealists seeking liberty, justice and brotherhood in the heart of darkness.

PART TWO

Between Two Worlds
1620-1621

Heigh Ho-o-o-o-o, Up she rises
Heigh Ho-o-o-o, Up she rises, early in the
   morning.
Whachu gonna do-o-o with a drunken sailor
Put him in the long boat and make him bail er
Earlee in the Morning
Heigh Ho up she rises
Heigh Ho-o-o up she rises
Earlee in the morning.

How Master Christopher Jones Brought the
"Mayflower" Across the Vast and Furious
Ocean Through Many and Divers Perils and
Came Upon Cape Cod

(September-November, 1620)

Up came the dripping anchor as the sailors
spun the capstan to the rhythm of the rousing
chanty.

The "Mayflower" slowly swung about, and her
sails filled with the light breeze. There was a waving of hats and scarfs. The rugged shore line faded
into a blue smudge on the horizon. The ship dipped
and rose as her brown sails tugged and billowed in
the spanking breeze.

Hungry-eyed, the "Mayflower's" passengers lingered at the rail feeding on the last sight of old England. One by one with tear-wet cheeks they turned away to the immediate crowded life and routine of shipboard.

Exploring youngsters were hauled out of the rigging and warned away from the ship's rails by scolding mothers. Sleeping quarters were assigned below decks and in the after cabins, and the routine of feeding a hundred passengers three times a day began. Seasick landlubbers gradually got their sea legs to navigate the rhythmic rise and fall of the ship's decks.

Each morning and evening the Pilgrims knelt together and fervently prayed, thanking God for his goodness and blessing. Devoutly they listened to the Bible reading of the Lord's Providence for his people on perilous seas, of Israel's crossing of the Red Sea, and of Noah, of Jonah and of Paul, and of how these passed safely through troubled waters.

Each day they watched the everchanging sky and the mysterious sea, always from the exact center of the great circle where they met on the horizon. Alongside, the porpoises played in gay parades, and sometimes the glistening backs and misty spoutings of a school of sperm whale could be seen. The foam broke in white plumes from the bluff bows of the "Mayflower" as she dipped her blunt nose into the mid-Atlantic swells, ever pushing into the West. In her wake a lacy green foam track stretched back toward England. From her mainmast the jaunty British merchant flag with its crosses of St. George and St. Andrew flashed in the sunlight.

Then the weather changed and worsened. The skies lowered and the wind rose into the wild autumn gales of the North Atlantic blowing out of the West. The ship lifted like a cork riding the heavy seas and plunged down vast mountainsides of water. She staggered under the blows of waves that washed over her decks. Beneath her keel and pushing back against her bows flowed the current of the then unknown Gulf Stream, moving eastward through the ocean.

The Leyden congregation was made up of devout Christians. If they prayed and spoke often the name of God, it was with deep reverence and gratitude. But the crew of the "Mayflower" were tough British sailors hardened in sin, and degraded by the brutal seafaring life of the time. They delighted in cursing the pious, blaspheming the name of God, and shouting foul language in the presence of the passengers till the women held their hands to their ears and the Pilgrim Elders shuddered. The best and the worst companioned on the heaving decks of the little ship on a long strange voyage.

A proud and very profane young seaman, the bitterest against them of all the wild crew, had mockingly said he hoped to help cast half of them overboard before they reached land. Soon after, he was smitten with a grievous malady and shortly died. As they solemnly consigned his body to the sea, both passengers and crew stood awed, believing that this was none other than the just hand of God upon his wickedness.

As the weather worsened, Master Jones ordered that in heavy seas all passengers must remain below decks. In spite of orders, young John Howland ventured out on the main deck in the midst of a violent gale. A great wave struck the ship and pitched him into the raging sea.

"Man overboard!" The shout was lost in the roar of the storm as the yellow head of John Howland disappeared in the furious waters. And then the incredible happened. As Howland went down,

his hand grasped the end of a rope that trailed over
the ship's side. When the ship rose on the next
wave, Howland, clinging desperately, was swung
against the ship's side. In a moment a boat hook had
been thrust through his leather jacket, and he was
hauled over the rail to safety. It was the hand of
God that reached out and saved him, said every
Pilgrim on the "Mayflower."

Day after day the staunch little ship held on—a speck in the violence of wind and water.

"The main beam has buckled, Sir!" shouted the first mate to the skipper standing at the half-deck rail.

Below decks they found where the cracked beam sagged under the weight of the main deck. A hurried council debated what to do. Another terrible blow from the seas might break the back of the ship.

"Better turn back," said the faint-hearted, "before she breaks up and goes to the bottom."

The passengers hauled out a great iron jack-screw which they had brought from Leyden, found a firm footing and slowly turned the screw until it bit into the oaken beam and slowly lifted it back to its proper place. A strong post set firm on the lower deck was put under it, and the huge beam was as stout as ever. Master Jones knew that his ship was strong and firm below the waterline. The upper works could be caulked well enough to keep out any dangerous amount of water. *"So they committed themselves to the will of God and resolved to procede."*

In the lull of the wind a shrill small crying could

be heard from the women's cabin. A Pilgrim baby had been born in the fury of the storm.

"We'll call him Oceanus," said the father, Stephen Hopkins. "He's a drop of the ocean, a sea pearl, a water baby—the youngest Pilgrim." Everyone thought it was a wonderful name.

Samuel Fuller, their surgeon from Leyden, had brought with him as servant a lad named William Butten. As the journey drew toward its end the boy sickened, and in spite of his master's profession, died. He was the only one of the passengers to do so on the crossing.

Land could not be far off. Master Jones had followed the forty-second parallel like a hen on a straight line. It was not possible to miss a whole continent. They must soon sight land after nine weeks at sea, he figured. Among the passengers there was a sense of excitement and anticipation. This was not an ordinary landing after a long voyage. There was a deep and strong feeling among them of something immense and heroic and biblical, beyond the personal happenings of their individual lives. They did not know what the ordeal might be ahead, only that they would never turn back. Something was being left behind forever.

Something new and bright and glorious was beginning. They were ready to face untold hardship. They were confident of wide new freedom. Vague, deep thoughts that could find no words drew them together in purpose and high resolve.

Christopher Jones was a shipmaster who ruled his crew with an iron hand, but he knew a man when he saw one, and he had learned to respect his strange passengers and their faith. A master craftsman of the sea, he had hunted whale in the Baltic, and had for years taken his ship across the Bay of Biscay laden deep with fragrant casks of Spanish wine. This was his first trip across the Atlantic, but with his compass and cross staff he could take his ship to any known destination across the seven seas of the round world with a clear head and a fearless heart. He had brought his ship safely across the vast North Atlantic, and he was relieved to think that he would soon disembark his hundred English passengers on the American continent and, he hoped, soon be on his way home to merry England.

Landfall

(November, 1620)

The sun rose red over the rim of the eastern horizon and tinted the sails of the "Mayflower" a delicate gold. Captain Jones sniffed the westward breeze, smelling the sweet smell of the land. Overside, the blue-black of deep water had turned to emerald green. After nine weeks of the wild Atlantic, land was overdue. The leadsman had found bottom at eighty fathoms, and now from the lookout at the maintop came the cry, "Land ho! Land ho-o-o-o-o!" The "Mayflower" had made a sixty-seven day crossing, covering about three thousand miles at an average speed of two miles an hour.

At once the whole ship came alive and into action. The passengers piled out of their bunks, hastily pulled on their clothing, rushed on deck, and crowded to the rail. Yes—there it was—a dark streak, with flecks of white cliff, running north and south as far as the eye could reach.

At the long-awaited sight of land, the women's faces became wet with tears, and the men stood silent with hearts too full for words. Kneeling on the deck for morning prayer, they thanked God

and sang *Old Hundredth* with a fervor they had never known before. Their eyes had seen the Promised Land.

In the ship's cabin Captain Jones explained that the land was not Virginia, but Cape Cod, many leagues to the north. They had come upon Cape Cod, the Master explained, a long bent finger that ran out into the Atlantic and beckoned toward Europe, calling to the Old World from the New.

But, said the Elders, their patent said Virginia. They had contracted with the company to take them to Virginia, and they insisted that the captain carry out the company's part of the bargain.

Very well, the "Mayflower" tacked about and ran due south. All day the passengers at the rail gazed curiously at the low-lying coast of Cape Cod.

As twilight came on, the wind died down. The ship had suddenly come in among shoals and breakers. They were in the perilous waters of a ships' graveyard, the broken part of Pollack's Rip, one of the most dangerous stretches of water on the New England coast. At any moment the treacherous currents might carry the ship upon the deadly shoals.

"Pray as you never prayed before," said Captain Jones to the Pilgrim Elders. Mercifully the wind sprang up from the south and filled the "Mayflower's" sails, slowly pulling her out of the shoals into deep water. She was safe.

As darkness fell, the Captain hove her to for the night. In the morning, the Pilgrims held a council in the cabin with the Captain. It seemed best to take advantage of the good south wind that had saved them and run north to anchor in Cape Cod Bay.

Next day, with a fair wind continuing from the south, the "Mayflower" ran up the coast. By nightfall they were off Race Point, the northernmost point of Cape Cod. Tomorrow, by God's grace, their ship would find anchorage.

There had been some glib talk that day among the "strangers" who came aboard at London and were not of the Congregation. These people had said that when the ship landed at Cape Cod, they would not be bound by the Virginia patent, and so would take orders from none, but would be their own masters.

"This," thought Elder Brewster that night, "is none other than the voice of Satan seeking to sow discord, trouble and mutiny among the Lord's people." He cast about in his mind for the wording of a compact. If the "Mayflower" passengers were not under the laws of Virginia, then they would make their own law, and agree to abide strictly by it.

Next morning the ship nosed into Provincetown harbor around the Long Point. After morning prayer, the passengers assembled 'tween decks to hear their Pastor's message. They stood silent and hushed in a solemn pause between two worlds: the Old World behind them and the New World on which they had not set foot.

Mr. Brewster stood up and said,

"It was thought good there should be an Association or Agreement, that we should combine together in one body; and to submit to such Government and Governors as we should, by common consent, agree to make and choose: and set our hands to this that follows, word for word."

In ye name of God, amen.

We whose names are underwriten,
the loyall subjects of our
dread soveraigne lord, King James,
by ye grace of God, of Great
Britaine,
France, & Ireland king,
defender of ye faith, &c.,
Haveing undertaken, for ye glorie of
God,
and advancemente of ye Christian faith
and honour of our king & countrie,
a voyage to plant ye first colonie
in ye Northerne parts of Virginia
Doe by these presents solemnly &
mutualy
in ye presence of God, and one of
another;
covenant, & combine ourselves
togeather
into a civill body politick; for our
better ordering, & preservation &
furtherance

of ye ends aforesaid; and by vertue
hearof
to enacte, constitute, and frame
such just & equall lawes, ordinances,
Acts,
constitutions, & offices, from time to
time,
as shall be thought most meete &
convinient
for ye generall good of ye colonie:
unto which we promise all due
submission
and obedience.

In witnes whereof we have
hereunder
subscribed our names at Cap-Codd
ye 11 of November in ye year of ye
raigne
of our soveraigne lord King James
of England, France, & Ireland
ye eighteenth and of Scotland ye
fiftie fourth.
Ano. Dom. 1620.

Of How the "Mayflower" Came to Anchor at Cape Cod and of How the Pilgrims Assayed a Voyage of Discovery and Found Goodly Stores of Indian Corn

(November, 1620)

The "Mayflower" had put her anchor down in Provincetown Harbor during a midmorning on a Saturday in November, 1620. White gulls screamed about the ship, and vast flocks of birds took wing along the shores. Inland the low hills were covered with goodly trees and the white beach stretched as far as the eye could see.

Because of shallow water, the ship could not come near shore by three-quarters of an English mile. "It is a harbor wherein a thousand sail of ships may ride!" wrote Mr. Winslow with delight.

Already that morning the forty-one had put their names to the compact. Every passenger was ready for action after nine weeks of idleness at sea.

At noon sixteen men went ashore in the longboat for wood and water and to explore what the land was. They had to wade the distance of a bow shot or two in the shallow water before they could beach the boat. Ashore they found springs of sweet water and filled their kegs. From the woods men brought back a boatload of fragrant juniper for the cook's fire.

The shallop brought from England would have been useful in traveling between ship and shore, but when she was examined she was found badly in need of repairs, a job for the ship's carpenter. Monday morning she was brought ashore and work on her started at once, but it was sixteen days before she could be made seaworthy.

In spite of this difficulty, the passengers were eager to feel the good earth under foot again. On Monday morning, the women loaded the longboat with soiled linen and went ashore to do their washing in fresh water.

"Be sure the Indians don't carry you off," said a sailor laughingly, as he helped a plump matron down the ship's ladder. "Though I'm thinking you would be making a toothsome dish for a cannibal chief," he added with a guffaw.

Captain Jones, who was leaning on the half-deck rail, found it hard not to smile at this, so he looked away. Lifting his eyes seaward, he saw a thin spout of vapor rising in the air.

"Thar she blows!" he called, as the black backs of a school of whales rose about the ship.

"Thar floats a good four-thousand-pounds' worth of sperm oil, if only we had the harpoons and tackle to take it," replied the mate wistfully.

The passengers crowded to the rail, marveling at the strange sea monsters as one whale, longer than the ship itself, came almost alongside. A young man hastily loaded a musket and aimed at the whale. There was a sudden explosion. The bursting gun barrel flew into splinters, knocking the man flat on the deck. The whale, with a sweep of his mighty tail, dove for the bottom of Cape Cod Bay.

When they picked up the dazed whale hunter, it was found that miraculously neither he nor anyone else had been injured by the explosion of the overcharged musket.

But there were more important things than shooting whales to be done. In order that no time be lost, on November 25th a party of sixteen goodly men volunteered under Captain Miles Standish to explore the coast for a place of settlement. Each man was given a sword, a musket and a steel corselet to protect his ribs against Indian arrows. The captain put on the steel helmet with nose and cheek guards that he had worn in the wars in Flanders.

In single file the company marched down the endless strip of beach toward the Unknown. Under his visor, the blue eyes of the Captain ranged the distance, alert and ready for danger, adventure and the unexpected in the mysterious land that lay before them.

Far ahead he saw a little group of figures advancing toward them on the beach. At first he thought they must be Master Jones and his men, who had gone ashore for wood. But as they came nearer there was no mistaking them. The figures were five naked Indians and a dog. The savages now saw them and stood still. As the Captain waved and shouted, the Indians turned and ran at top speed back down the beach.

The Englishmen followed on the run, but because of their heavy guns and armor, they were soon outdistanced by the racing Indians. For ten miles the Englishmen followed their footprints until they turned off into the woods.

At last darkness overtook them, so they built a barricade of logs and brush, and ate their biscuits and cheese by a roaring fire. It was their first night in the wilderness, so the Captain posted three sentinels, and the rest of the men lay down by their muskets. Soon the weary men were all asleep.

In the dawn they kneeled and prayed, breakfasted and marched on into the woods. For hours the discoverers struggled on through the thick brush that tore at their clothes and armor, but they found no trace of Indians. Exhausted and thirsty, they followed deer paths down a steep valley. There they threw themselves down by a cool spring of fresh water.

"And drank our first New England water with as much delight as ever we drank drink in all our lives."

Farther on they came upon a clear pond of fresh water (Pond Village in Truro) where the deer came to drink, and along the banks were flocks of water fowl.

In an open field they found new stubble where the Indians had grown corn. Near by were some old boards where an Indian lodge had been and by it an iron ship's kettle. Each find hinted of a strange story about the mysterious people of the forest. Near by was a newly made mound of sand marked with the print of hands. Under it they found a little old basket of gleaming Indian corn.

Perhaps even now, they thought, the unseen people were watching them from the forests. Sentinels stood watch as the discoverers began to dig about the Indian mounds. They uncovered a large new basket beautifully woven and took out thirty-six ears of red and golden corn. The basket held three or four bushels of corn. This was a treasure more precious than gold to men who would have to get their food from this very soil. The men filled the iron kettle and their pockets with corn and buried the rest till they would come again.

Marching on, they came to a river (Pamet Harbor) where they found two Indian canoes cleverly made of bark. As it was time to return, they followed their trail back to the Fresh Water Ponds and made their barricaded camp. They slept from weariness in the cold rain, while three sentinels kept watch through the night.

Next morning, after fighting their way through the entangling underbrush, they became aware that they were lost in the forest. In the woods ahead, Stephen Hopkins was calling. When the party came up, he pointed to a bent sapling with a cord and noose cunningly made and set in a deer path about a bait of acorns.

"It is how the Indians catch deer!" said Stephen.

As William Bradford stepped forward to examine it, the sapling gave a jerk, and he found himself suddenly hanging by one leg upside down. The woods rang with laughter as he was released from the trap and set upon his feet.

They soon came out on the beach where they sighted the "Mayflower." They fired off their muskets and were welcomed home by Masters Jones and Carver, who were waiting on shore with the longboat.

"And thus we came, both weary and welcome, home; and delivered our corn into the store, to be kept for seed; for we knew not how to come by any, and therefore were very glad; purposing soon as we could meet with any of the inhabitants of that place, to make them large satisfaction.

*"*THIS WAS OUR FIRST DISCOVERY."

Of the Adventure in the Shallop and of the Mystery of the Blond Skull

It was late November and the bleak northern winter was upon them. Landward lay the unknown wilderness where they must soon find a place for their settlement. The shallop was now seaworthy and ready to take the expedition down the Cape. Master Jones was made the leader of a party that would search for a good site. It consisted of ten sailors and twenty-four men from among the passengers.

As the shallop ran down the coast through a wild sea, it blew bitter cold with snow. The spray froze to the men's clothing till they were covered with ice. A landing party went ashore at the place of the First Discovery, which they called appropriately Cold Harbour (the Pamet River). All day they marched up and down through the rugged snow-covered hills.

That night the hungry marchers feasted under the pines on three fat geese and six ducks they had killed. They slept in the snow by a fragrant juniper fire under a windward barricade.

Next morning they crossed the river in an abandoned Indian canoe and found the place where they had dug up the baskets of corn (Hopkins' Cliff). Again they dug, breaking through the frozen ground with their cutlasses and levers until they found ten more baskets of precious seed corn.

"AND SURE IT WAS GOD'S PROVIDENCE THAT WE FOUND THIS CORN; FOR ELSE WE KNOW NOT HOW WE SHOULD HAVE DONE."

More bad weather was coming and Master Jones grew anxious for his ship, so he went back with the sick members of the party and the baskets of corn. Before he left, he promised to return next day with spades and mattocks.

The eighteen men who remained pushed on through the woods, finding a broad path that they thought might lead to an Indian village. The musketeers lighted their match cords to be ready for action, but the road proved to be only a deer path leading nowhere.

As they came out of the woods on open, level ground, the men found old boards heaped on a long mound that looked like a grave. Digging down, they unearthed rush mats, bowls, trays, and dishes, a bow and a painted and carved stick, then a new mat, and under that two bundles. In the larger bundle, wrapped in a sailor's blouse and breeches, were the bones and skull of a man. The skull had strands of fine yellow hair still on it and some of the flesh unconsumed.

The discoverers looked at one another in wonder. What was the mystery behind this blond skull in the bottom of a lonely Indian grave on desolate Cape Cod?

Had this white man been a great chief, or was he a shipwrecked sailor who had been murdered?

What strange tales about the wilderness, as it was before the "Mayflower" came, could these bones tell? In the other bundle were the bones of a child with wampum necklaces and bracelets. The men took some of the trinkets and covered the graves.

Then they made another discovery: two round lodges, scarcely visible under the blanket of snow. Inside the lodges were all the objects of an Indian household, including finely woven mats and earthen pots that had recently been in use. The discoverers took away what they fancied and, as it was growing dark, they hurried down to the shore, went aboard the shallop, and reached the "Mayflower" that night.

As the men told of their adventures and of the mystery of the Blond Skull, Elder Brewster's Christian conscience twitched uneasily. They had robbed the Indian graves and stolen the natives' corn, but he promised himself that

"As soon as we can meet with them, we will give them full satisfaction.

"THUS MUCH FOR OUR SECOND DISCOVERY."

Of the Third Discovery and of the First Encounter and of Divers Perils by Land and Sea

(December, 1620)

November had passed. Winter lay over the Cape and the weather worsened. Each day there were fewer provisions. The sailors aboard the "Mayflower" were impatient to start on the return voyage to England. The Pilgrims were anxious to find a safe harbor and a good place to build a settlement.

Robert Coppin, the ship's pilot, said he could take them to a good harbor across the bay where he had been on a previous voyage. The place was called Thieves' Harbor because an Indian had there stolen a harpoon from them.

For a second time the shallop put off from the "Mayflower" and ran down the Cape coast before a stiff east wind that blew ever colder. The sea spray froze in the men's beards. Miles Standish and his musketeers wrapped their heavy cloaks around their muskets to keep them dry. Brewster and Carver huddled in the stern and the pilot, Coppin, manned the tiller. In all there were sixteen men. Two seasick men hung limply over the gunwales.

After a twenty-mile run they came to a sandy point of land running out into the Bay (Billingsgate Point) and found a fair harbor (Wellfleet Bay). As the sailors sought to make a landing among the sand flats, they spied, away down the beach, a little group of figures crowded around some dark object. When the seamen hailed them, they quickly disappeared into the woods.

Wading over the sand flats, the discoverers came ashore and built a landward barricade and a fire. Five miles inland they saw a smoke column rise in the evening sky from an Indian signal fire. The Indians had seen them and were warning their people. By this time, the discoverers were too tired to worry about the redmen, so after a lean supper they slept on the frozen ground.

In the morning the party divided, some going in the shallop to explore the coast and the rest marching inland to seek a suitable place of settlement.

In the sea wash along the beach they came upon the fifteen-foot body of a strange sea creature. "It is a kind of whale called a Grampus," said Coppin, cutting a strip of flesh with his knife from the carcass. It was two inches thick of solid fat.

Farther down the beach they found another Grampus half stripped of his coat of fat. The sand about the creatures body was printed with the feet of the Indians the men had seen from the boat. "We will call this place Grampus Bay," said Captain Standish.

All day the men ranged over the rough country seeking a site for their New World home, but they found none. Their exploring was not useless, however, for it taught them one thing. Old corn fields, abandoned lodges, and a melancholy Indian cemetery, surrounded by a high palisade, were evidence enough that the mysterious Indians were near.

As the red sun sank in the gray west, the discoverers marched wearily back to the sea coast. Thank heaven they could see the brown sail of the shallop standing off shore!

As they made camp, there was a cheerful feeling in finding one another safe again. After warming their numb hands at the juniper fire behind the rough barricade, they ate their bit of cheese and biscuit. Soon they were asleep with their muskets under their cloaks.

It seemed they had hardly closed their eyes when a voice roused them. "Wake up, Captain! The Indians be upon us." The sentinel was shaking Standish violently by the shoulder. "To arms, to arms!"

The cry brought every man to his feet in a moment. From the woods came a high-pitched yell in a wild inhuman cadence. The sentinels fired a couple of musket shots toward the sound, and the crying suddenly ceased.

"It's only the song of the wild wolves," muttered a seaman, who had met wolves before in Newfoundland.

The fire was built up, a sentinel added to the watch, and they slept on uneasily through the night.

Before dawn the men turned out and knelt in a circle while Brewster said the morning prayers. As the cook prepared breakfast, several men took their muskets down to the shore, where they left them till the shallop should come in on the tide.

Suddenly a chorus of wild yells burst from the land side. It was the same yelping cries they had heard at midnight, but this time there was no mistaking the terrible Indian war cry. A shower of arrows fell around the campfire.

The four men at the barricade who had kept their muskets, lighted their fuses at the fire, while the rest ran for the shore where they had left their firearms. Several shadowy figures broke from the woods in pursuit, and then turned and ran, as a half dozen soldiers armed with cutlasses charged out from behind the barricade.

Captain Standish called to the shallop and the heartening cry came back, "Well, well. Be of good courage," as the sailors fired two or three shots. Then someone called from the shallop for a firebrand to light their match cords. A soldier picked a brand from the fire and ran down to the shallop. Arrows showered on the barricade and the war cries rose louder.

In the dim light, the men firing from the barricade could see a huge Indian behind the nearest tree. As the bullets whizzed about him, he kept coolly shooting his bow, till a shot hit the tree and sent splinters flying about his head. He gave a terrific yell and ran as the whole band vanished into

the forest. The Englishmen followed them for a quarter mile, keeping up the firing.

The fight was over. The men came back and gathered up the arrows to send to England as a grim souvenir of how things were in New England.

"*Yet by the special Providence of God none of them either hit, or hurt, us: though many came close by us, and on every side of us, and some coats which hung up in our barricado were shot through and through.*

"*So after we had given God thanks for our deliverance; we took our shallop, and went on our journey; and called this place THE FIRST ENCOUNTER.*"

(The location was the present Eastham.)

How the Discoverers Sought Thievish Bay and Found Plymouth Harbor and a Goodly Situation

(December, 1620)

The First Encounter was not the greatest battle of history, but for the hatters and weavers of Leyden it was a fiery baptism in peril and danger. As they sat in the shallop running before the wind, they recounted to one another all the excitements of their great adventure.

By mid-afternoon the shallop was bucking the rough sea like a wild horse and the wind bellying her sail in a full arc. It began to rain. Then the rain changed to snow. A great wave tore off the shallop's rudder, leaving the tiller useless in Pilot Coppin's hands. Two seamen grabbed up oars and held the little boat desperately on her course. The wind rose until the straining mast cracked and broke in three places.

For a few desperate moments it seemed that the shallop would capsize, but the seamen cut loose the tangle of sail and tackle and she slowly righted herself.

"Good cheer, my hearties," shouted Coppin. "I can see the harbor, and we shall soon be in."

As the shallop came in to shore on the tide and wind, they could see the breakers dashing against the rocky cove. Coppin peered through the dusk. He realized he was mistaken and confused.

"So help me, I've never seen this place before," he muttered. "Run her ashore before the wind," he called to the mate.

The shallop now was rapidly drifting toward where the booming surf broke on the rocks. But the sailors at the steering oars brought her about and someone shouted, "If you are men, row lustily, or we are lost."

The men bent to the oars and the shallop slowly pulled up into the wind and out of the churning surf toward the open water. Rowing on through the dark and the rain in the teeth of a northeaster, presently they pulled in under a dark mass of rock that sheltered them from the bitter winds. Here they anchored for the night.

At midnight the wind changed, and it froze hard. The men in the shallop shivered through the long night. In the gray of dawn three or four men went ashore with the cold in their bones, to build a fire. With much coaxing, the damp wood at last took fire, and soon the storm-tossed discoverers were warming their hands around a driftwood fire.

After prayers of thanks for deliverance, and breakfast, they explored the wooded island all day and found they were safe from the Indians.

Next morning the sun rose brilliantly out of the Bay in a clear sky. The men dried the sea water out of their shirts, put their guns in order, and rested from the wildness of the sea.

It being Sunday, December 20th, the Pilgrims

kept the Sabbath in prayer and in listening to Mr. Brewster's discourse, but the sea-weary sailors snored godlessly around the fire.

"*On Monday they sounded the harbor and found it fit for shipping; and marched into the land and found diverse cornfields, and little running brooks, a place (as they supposed) fit for situation; at least it was ye best they could find, and ye season & their present necessity made them glad to accepte of it. So they returned to their shipp againe with this news to ye rest of their people which did much comforte their harts.*"

The Third Discovery had brought back encouraging news of the good harbor at Plymouth. But tragic news awaited Bradford aboard the "Mayflower." In his absence his beloved wife, Dorothy, had been drowned. She had fallen overboard in the storm on the day after he had left. He remembered how she had waved him a brave farewell. He had never guessed what fears had filled her heart as she had gazed at the bleak coast to which they had so perilously come. They had hoped and planned for a new life together in the wilderness, but now he must go on alone. In time William turned from his dark thoughts and threw himself into the days of toil and danger that lay ahead.

New life as well as death had come aboard the "Mayflower." A fine baby boy had been born to Mistress Susanna White. He was the first English baby born in New England. They gave him the name of Peregrine, or the Wanderer. In spite of his name, he spent the eighty-odd years of a hard-working life without ever leaving New England.

Of How the "Mayflower" Came to Plymouth Harbor and of How They Built Their Towne and of the Cruel Sickness That Came Upon Them

(December, 1620)

It was mid-December when the "Mayflower" weighed anchor and sailed across Cape Cod Bay. When she came within six miles of the mainland, the wind changed and she had to beat out to sea again.

Next day, the wind being fair, she came into

Plymouth Harbor and anchored about a mile and a half off shore. Because of the shallow water, she could get no nearer. The passengers had to ferry from ship to shore through the stormy waters all winter long.

"This Bay is a most hopeful place," said Mr. Winslow as they came ashore in the shallop to seek a "situation," or place to settle. As they explored inland they studied the lay of the land, sampled the soil, carefully noted the positions of springs and brooks, and considered the possibilities of Indian attack from the surrounding forest.

From the hilltop above the Harbor they could look to the seaward horizon and landward across the wooded hills to the sunset. It would be an excellent place for a fort protecting the seaward slope. On this slope they planned to build their houses. A brook of sweet water ran down beside it, and south of it were old Indian cornfields.

They made their decision to settle in this place by vote in the democratic English way. Here by the abundant bay, at long last they would build. This would be their home and haven of rest after many storm-blown wanderings.

Between the sinister forests and the bay they

would build a New England with their naked hands and a few tools, with sweat and tears and heartache.

Before starting to build, they planned well. The congregation was separated into nineteen families. Then along a street that led from the hill to the water's edge, the hill slope was divided into plots. The families drew lots for their location. John Carver, who had been their leader aboard the "Mayflower," was confirmed as Governor for the coming year.

Twenty men remained ashore in a barricaded camp and began cutting timber for building. The rest lived on the "Mayflower" and went back and forth from the ship to their day's work ashore.

On Christmas Day they worked on the common house, or shelter, which was for storing provisions, ammunition, and clothing. All that day the axes swung. At night the weary builders went back to the ship, leaving twenty men ashore. Between decks on the "Mayflower" they ate a meager dinner with British cheer. Then they sang the old carols, with their hearts back again in merry England, as a storm lashed through the rigging of the "Mayflower" in Plymouth Harbor.

As the winter wore on, hacking coughs and fever and scurvy began to take their toll among the passengers. But whenever the rain and sleet died down, the men who could walk at all went ashore to work on the common house. They began the platform of the fort and the family dwellings along the new street.

When the common house was thatched, provisions and ammunition were brought ashore and stored in it. In the remaining space, the sick beds lay end to end. Here among the stricken lay Bradford and Carver.

One day a spark caught in the dry thatch of the common house, and its roof took fire. At the cries of alarm, the workmen rushed to the burning building and carried out the sick. Before the fire was checked, food and precious stores were damaged, but by the grace of God no lives were lost.

From the top of the Mount, Miles Standish gazed grimly across the pine-clad hills in the west to where columns of smoke rose against the gray sky from Indian signal fires.

For this thing called Freedom, Standish now well knew, there was a price to pay. Below him in the village, death had taken nearly half of the peo-

MILES STANDISH

ple. Rose Standish, his wife, was among the first who had died. He had knelt at her side at the last hour. He would rather have taken an arrow through his heart. Fourteen of the eighteen Pilgrim wives had died. They had been buried at night in unmarked graves, so that the savages should not know how few remained. Sometimes there were two or three deaths in a day.

He and a half dozen others still had strength enough to feed the thin soup to the sick, to cheer the wasted forms in the crude beds, to hew wood and carry water so that Plymouth might live.

Bradford from his sick bed had watched the stocky man of war, day and night on his rounds, tending the sick with a woman's tenderness. Years later, rugged old Governor Bradford remembered and wrote tribute in his blunt prose.

"There was but 6 or 7 sound persons, so to their great comendations be it spoken, spared no pains, night or day, but with abundance of toyle and hazard of their owne health, fetched them woode, made them fires, drest them meat, made their beads, washed their lothsome cloaths, cloathed and uncloathed them; in a word did

all ye homly and necessarie offices for them which dainty & quesie stomacks can not endure to hear named; & all this willingly and cherfully, without any grudging in ye least, shewing herein their true love unto their friends & brethern. A rare example and worthy to be remembered. Tow of these 7 were Mr. William Brewster, ther Reverend Elder and Miles Standish ther Captein and military commander, unto whom myself & many others, were much holden in our low & sicke condition."

Death had come aboard the "Mayflower." One by one the sickness took the riotous crew who brutally ignored their comrades dying miserably in their bunks. To these men who had cursed and tormented them, the women aboard the ship brought what care and comfort they could with a Christlike compassion.

In the fires and ice of that first winter, their spirits were steel-tempered to build a nation of men and women who would never turn back in quest of freedom and justice and of brotherhood.

Lost in the Forest
(January, 1621)

To those city dwellers from Leyden who for years had lived sheltered indoor lives, this rugged existence on the bleak New England hillside was utterly new and strange. Around and enclosing them stretched the mysterious forest. As they wandered into it in search of food or wood, unforeseen adventures suddenly beset them. Terrifying situations for which they were utterly unprepared overtook them.

To men who had spent drab and colorless years

at the looms of Leyden, each day in this strange world brought dangers, violent actions, and sudden challenges.

One day at noon four thatch cutters stopped work and got out their biscuit and cheese for dinner. After they had finished their simple meal, Peter Browne and John Goodman decided to walk in the woods towards the lakes with their two dogs.

When Peter and John did not return, their companions searched the woods calling and hallooing, but no trace of the men or dogs was to be found. Maybe Peter and John had walked into an Indian ambush. The two searchers hurried back to the Plantation with the news. All that afternoon a search party scoured the woods, but found no trace of the two men. Next day a dozen musketeers ranged as far as they dared into the forest, but they had no success.

The truth of the matter was that Peter and John had walked deep into the forest. Their two dogs, a little spaniel and a mastiff, had run ahead, sniffing among the leaves. Suddenly the dogs made a dash through the thicket towards the lake shore, and a great buck leaped lightly up and away. The chase was on. Peter and John ran excitedly after the dogs.

This was a rare chance for venison for hungry Plymouth.

The deer had vanished as if it had been on wings, but the dogs went rushing noisily through the brush. After an hour's chase the two men became winded, and called back their animals. As Peter and John tramped back among the bare tree trunks, they became bewildered and called and called until they were hoarse. They were lost; even the dogs could not pick up their trail back. As the early winter twilight came on, it began to rain. The men were fagged and very hungry. Soon the wind blew cold and snow began to fall. Utterly bewildered, they staggered on. Through the darkness a long and dismal howl rose and then another. It seemed to follow them.

"It must be lions," said Peter, who knew very little about animals.

The two men found a tree that they could easily climb. Very near them another long howl wavered through the night.

"It *is* a lion," said John, who knew even less about zoology.

The spaniel whimpered and the mastiff strained at her leash as the hair on her neck bristled, but the men held her back. When "the lions" came Peter and John planned to let her go while they themselves took to the tree. All that night they paced up and down in the snow and freezing cold, numb and unspeakably miserable.

Dawn came and the howling ceased. They marched on through the snow. All morning they dragged on. That afternoon, after they crossed a five-mile plain that had been burnt off by the Indians, they came to a hill. From its top they caught a gleam of light on water. It was Plymouth Harbor! They could make out the island and the long fish-hook peninsula. They staggered into the Plantation half frozen and exhausted, but still alive.

A week later John Goodman hobbled out for a walk on his lame feet, with the little spaniel for a companion. Two gray wolves leaped from a thicket and ran for the spaniel. The little dog dashed back to safety between John Goodman's legs.

As the wolves circled, John heaved a log that struck one brute, and the wolves ran off. In a few minutes they were back. John brandished a sharp stake he had found. The wolves drew off and sat on their haunches grinning hungrily at the trembling spaniel. John himself was terribly shaky in the knees, but he stood his ground and dared the wolves to come on. Presently they slunk off over the snow and disappeared in the woods.

The Plantation was a little island of safety in the threatening wilderness. Outside its palisade lay the vast unknown, the threatening forest, the wolves, the lurking Indians, the daily battle with cold and hunger and danger. But bright or dim, the light of faith and courage burned steadily and unfailingly through the short grey days and long winter nights in the seven houses clustered on the hillside by Plymouth Harbor.

How the Spring Came and How Samoset Came Out of the Forest

(March, 1621)

Spring comes slowly to New England, but the March sun rose higher in the south and filled the land with brightness. The sick rose from their beds, grew stronger daily, and set about their labors. Fifty-one survivors were slowly coming back to life.

Little birds broke into song among the new leaves, the skunk cabbage and the jack-in-the-pulpit sprang greenly by the brook and the sound of spring thunder was heard. Women and children planted seeds in Plymouth gardens.

On such a spring day, a hunter came with news. While he had been crouching in the bushes by the creekside to bag a brace of ducks, twelve Indians had passed by toward Plymouth. In the woods he had heard many more. Miles Standish and Francis Cooke had left their tools in the forest. When they returned, their axes were gone. They could see Indian smoke signals and, silhouetted against the sky on a hilltop, two Indians signaled to them to come. When Standish and Cooke crossed the brook and laid down their muskets in sign of peace, the Indians disappeared.

Captain Jones brought their five cannons ashore, three heavy pieces and two little "basses." These were hauled lustily up the Mount and stationed on the unfinished gun platform. The people of Plymouth felt a lot safer as they looked toward the Indian smoke signals rising behind Watson Hill.

On March 26, 1621, the Plymouth Assembly was in morning session at the common house. Miles Standish had just been made officially their military commander.

Suddenly the door to the assembly room was pushed open and a tall Indian boldly entered. Everyone jumped up. "Welcome, English," said the savage. "Me Samoset." Then he added coolly, "Me want beer."

For the first time the amazed Englishmen were looking at an American Indian face to face. They gave him a glass of brandy, cheese and crackers, and some roast duck. The room was now crowded with neighbors wanting to see the Indian.

All afternoon Samoset answered questions in English—such as it was. He said that the English had settled on the lands of the Patuxet Indians; and that this tribe had been wiped out by the plague four years ago.

Samoset disclosed that the Indians who had attacked the exploring expedition at The First Encounter were the Nausites. Eight months before, this tribe had killed three Englishmen in a fight with Sir Fernando Gorges' party. The Nausites hated the English because a shipmaster named Hunt had kidnaped a number of their people under pretext of bartering with them. Hunt had then sold them into slavery in Spain.

Samoset himself had learned English from the fishermen who came each year to fish off the Banks, and he knew their captains by name. He told the names, numbers, and chiefs of neighboring tribes. The Elders were suspicious of Samoset as an overnight guest. However, he did not want to leave, so he was lodged at Stephen Hopkins' house where he slept peacefully on the bare floor.

Next morning, after giving Samoset a knife, a bracelet, and a ring, the Elders bade him farewell. They rejoiced that at last they had made an intelligent and valuable friend, and that great good must come of it.

Of the Visit of That Great Chief Massasoit and of the Lasting Peace and Friendship That Was Made Between Them

Next day (March 28th) was the Lord's Day in Plymouth. That afternoon Samoset strode down the Street with five tall savages behind him. They wore deerskin cloaks and leggings of the same material. In their black hair were eagle feathers and fox tails and their faces were painted black. They had left their bows and arrows outside the palisade. With them they brought the tools that Miles Standish had left in the forest. The braves ate very heartily of what the Elders provided and in return danced and sang for the amazed Pilgrims.

The Indians had come to barter, but Mr. Brewster explained that it was not the Pilgrims' custom on the Lord's Day. If the Indians would come again, with many beaver skins, the Plymouth folk would be glad to trade. So they gave the redmen bright trinkets and sent them back to the forest with an armed escort.

March 31st was a special day in the Plantation because the storm-damaged shallop was repaired and Captain Jones brought to land the last boatload of passengers from the "Mayflower." It had been just three months since the first Pilgrims landed.

A few days later Samoset again appeared at the door of the meeting house. He brought with him his friend Tisquantum, or Squanto. He was the last of the Patuxets and spoke English. He had been taken captive by Hunt and sold in Spain. Later, Squanto had lived in England and had finally come home to the tragic scene where the last of his people had perished.

After introducing Squanto, Samoset announced that the great Chief Massasoit and his brother Quadequina, with sixty warriors, were waiting on a nearby hilltop to council with the English.

Edward Winslow was sent with presents of food

SQUANTO

and brandy to greet them. He told the Chief that King James saluted Massasoit as his friend and ally, and that Governor Carver wished to make peace and to barter with the great Chief, his neighbor. Winslow invited him to come to their Plantation.

Captain Standish and a guard of musketeers met Chief Massasoit and his twenty braves at the town brook and escorted him to an unfinished house. Here Massasoit was seated in state on a green rug and colored cushions. Governor Carver now came to meet him followed by a drummer and trumpeter playing bravely. The rest of the Plymouth musketeers completed the parade.

The Chief was a superb figure of a man. His grave countenance was painted vermilion and his scalp lock decorated with feathers. The bodies of his warriors were painted with ceremonial decorations in black, red, white, and yellow.

Carver solemnly bent to kiss the Indian Chief's hand. When they all sat down Massasoit was presented with a mug of brandy. As the fiery liquid went down the Chief's throat, he shuddered and presently broke into a sweat.

Point by point Samoset translated for Massasoit the seven articles of the peace treaty and mutual alliance. The words danced dizzily through the fumes of the Dutch brandy in the Chief's befuddled brain.

In effect the treaty stated that:

1. There should be no aggression against each other.
2. Indians who damaged the English were to be turned over for punishment.
3. Stolen goods were to be returned. This was to apply to both Indians and English.
4. Each party would help the other in case either was attacked.
5. Massasoit should notify neighboring tribes of the defense pact and invite them to join.
6. Each party when visiting the other would leave his weapons behind.
7. Under these conditions King James would esteem Massasoit his friend and ally.

After Massasoit had somewhat shakily put his mark to the treaty, there was good-humored visiting. The Chief was much impressed with the Governor's trumpet and his warriors tried in vain to make it speak. On the Chief's departure, Governor Carver in person escorted him to the brook.

During the meeting, Winslow had remained with the Indians on the hill as a hostage. In like manner, the English had kept half a dozen savages.

Quadequina, the Chief's brother, now came down to Plymouth to be entertained. That night the English kept close watch just to see if the peace would really stick. But as the days passed and their woodsmen and hunters came back unharmed from the forest, they were certain that the Chief would keep faith. This treaty stood unbroken for fifty years.

A few days later Squanto created a sensation by bringing to Plymouth a mess of fat eels, which he had procured by treading them out of the mud with his feet. This trick he willingly taught the younger members of the colony, who soon became his friends and admirers. Squanto led them to the best fishing grounds and clam beds, showed them how to plant a fat herring in each corn hill to make the stalks grow tall and bear full golden ears, how to make snares and traps, and where the deer herds grazed, and where the fat turkey fed among the berry bushes.

PART THREE

New England Adventure
1621-1623

The Return of the "Mayflower"

(March-April, 1621)

THROUGH THE WINTER, THE WEATHER-BEATEN "Mayflower" had served as a base while the Pilgrims worked ashore on their houses and shelters. When the common house burned, the ship was a refuge for the homeless. In the first sickness, it had served as a hospital. In case of Indian attack, they looked to it for safety.

Now April was at hand and the surviving sailors were strong enough to work the ship on her long voyage back to England. With the "Mayflower" gone, the little settlement would be left without this island of safety, this last link to home.

A cannon shot from the ship sounded across the harbor. It was the signal for the ship's departure. Fifty-one gaunt men, women and children crowded to the shore where the ship's longboat waited. Captain Jones said the wind and tide were right. The hour had come to sail. For the last time, he offered to take aboard any who wished to return. No one answered. For many months, the Captain had lived with these people and had learned the stuff they were made of. He was not surprised.

He put their letters and packages in his leather bag. Bidding them all farewell, he returned to the ship.

Those left behind stood in silent little groups at the water's edge, their gaze fixed on the bright speck of sail fading on the horizon. At this moment their hearts were in old England in the sweet springtime.

As the "Mayflower" disappeared, they turned back to the rugged New England hillside. Each one knew that a greater gulf than the Atlantic separated them forever from the past. They had put their hand to the plow and did not look back.

All through that spring, both men and women worked daily in the fields and woods from dawn to dusk. Even their Governor Carver did the same hard labor as the rest. On a warm April day, while working in the fields, he was taken suddenly ill and lost consciousness. In a few days he died.

The colonists met and chose William Bradford for Governor. Bradford bravely took up the task and did his work well. For nearly thirty-five years he was elected Governor of new Plymouth. On his shoulders now rested the success of the colony. He made the rules, administered justice, divided the common store of provisions, and each

year allotted shares of the common land to each of the families. He also supervised the Indian trade and dealt with strangers according to their deserts. Because Bradford was still weak from the first sickness, Mr. Allerton was chosen as his assistant.

How Mr. Winslow Brought a Scarlet Coat to Massasoit and of Their Strange Entertainment by That Great Sagamore

(July, 1621)

Mrs. Hopkins was bending over the open fireplace. She was extracting a corn pudding from the pot that hung over the fire. This New England dish, which she herself had invented, was made of Indian corn and deer fat, with whatever seasoning happened to be at hand.

An uneasy feeling caused her to look round suddenly. "Wahoooo!" she yelled, dropping the pudding in the ashes. In the room stood a tall half-naked Indian making the peace sign. Behind him was a black-eyed squaw and two very naked little Indian boys. The Indian grinned, making friendly gestures.

"Lord, I never can get used to 'em," Mrs. Hopkins said, shaking her head, but making a kindly sign toward her visitors. "The way they creep up on you without making a sound! It's enough to scare the life out of a body. Thank the Lord they don't mean no harm."

The Indians were examining everything in the room. Mrs. Hopkins rescued the corn pudding from the ashes. "Here, taste this and be gone," she said, as she distributed slices of the pudding to her visitors and shooed them laughingly out of the door. "I've no time to waste this morning."

Little by little, the people of Plymouth were getting used to such visits. Singly or in groups, Indian visitors came out of the forest. Sometimes a dozen at a time came with their women, children and dogs. They arrived at all hours of the day to sit and talk, to trade, to smoke and eat. The English had little food or time to spare, and the Indians expected to be fed and entertained. These amiable visitors interrupted work, wasted time, became pests and nuisances.

Squanto alone had made himself useful. In fact he had become necessary in many different ways. Above all, he was "the tongue of the English." He became their official interpreter and lived in Plymouth.

When the planting was finished, Governor Bradford and his Council decided that it would be in the interests of peace and good business to return Massasoit's visits. Winslow was appointed as their ambassador to the great chief. He would take with him Squanto for guide and interpreter and John Hopkins, who was a very good shot. They would of course take along a present worthy of the great chief.

"A scarlet coat trimmed in lace is a vanity," observed the Governor, as he took the cotton hunting coat from the oaken chest and handed it to Winslow. "But methinks it will delight the heart of our new friend, Chief Massasoit. Remind him of our deep love and of our desire that he bring many more of the skins of the beaver to trade for mirrors and iron kettles. Explain kindly how we wish that his people would come less often to visit us, but assure him that *his* royal person will be always welcome. Beseech him that he search out those from whom we took their corn, that we may restore the same to them in full measure."

They started at sunrise, marching steadily through the green woods in single file, behind the silent Squanto. In the middle of the afternoon they sighted the smoke of a campfire and came upon a band of Indians in an open corn field. Squanto said they were a tribe called Namasheucks.

These Indians invited the English to eat with them. The hungry white men feasted on large helpings of corn bread and shad roe. This last novelty was the most delicious Indian food they had yet tasted.

Suddenly the Indians pointed excitedly to where a flock of crows were alighting in their field of young corn.

"They want you to shoot at the crows which are damaging their crops," Squanto explained.

Obligingly, Hopkins rested the heavy musket on the firing staff and took aim.

"Make sure you bring down the black thief," whispered Winslow.

The next second the shot resounded across the clearing, and the crows rose cawing with a great flapping of wings. The Indians ran and picked up the dead crow, amazed at the magic powers of the white hunter.

Squanto urged that the party push on while it was still light. After an eight-mile march, they came upon a fair river, where there were Indians taking fish. They had made a fine catch of bass. That night, the English and Indians feasted on fish fresh from the river. Then they slept under the stars, for the Indians had built no lodges here.

When Squanto and the Englishmen started off the next morning, six tall braves accompanied them. During the long hot day's march, the Indians carried the Englishmen's guns and baggage for them and took them over streams on their backs. The English admired the many kinds of fine trees as they marched through the forests. In places they crossed rough outcroppings of rock.

Once or twice the party met an Indian and his family and stopped to trade trinkets for food.

Along the rivers were the barren corn fields. These had been cultivated a few years before by a numerous tribe which had been wiped out by the plague. Winslow and his men came upon their skulls and bones lying in the underbrush.

Late in the day the party came out upon a river and Squanto pointed to where a village of round lodges straggled along the river bank.

"Here Massasoit and his people dwell," said Squanto.

Curious Indians surrounded the newcomers. When it was discovered that Massasoit was not there, a messenger was sent to notify him of Winslow's arrival.

Squanto urged that when Massasoit came the English should fire their muskets in his honor. The Chief was considerably startled by the salute and most of his people vanished into the woods. He was vastly pleased, however, when his visitors put the scarlet coat on his shoulders and a copper chain about his neck. He strutted about the village before his admiring subjects.

When he tired of this, Massasoit made a solemn

THE SCARLET COAT

speech, saying he agreed to all that the English desired. He would give them new varieties of seed corn. He asked only that they destroy his enemies, the terrible Narragansetts.

After the speech, he explained that he could not offer supper to his English visitors as he had procured no food, but he invited them to sleep in his lodge. Then, for entertainment, the tribe sang and danced till late in the night, while the hungry white men slapped at the mosquitoes.

That night in the Chief's lodge, they shared the hard board bed with Massasoit and his wife. Two more huge Indians crowded in beside them. The night was sultry and the lodge full of hungry fleas.

"We were worse weary of our lodging than of our journey," said Winslow.

Next day, the village was crowded with curious braves, their women, children, and dogs. They came for their first look at white men. Massasoit proudly paraded in his red coat. The Indians begged the white men to shoot at a mark. Hopkins blazed away at a dead tree with a charge of birdshot. The braves were amazed and puzzled to find the tree full of holes.

Later, for supper, Massasoit brought in two large

fish he had shot with his bow and arrows, but these did not go far among forty Indians. Their chief amusement was gambling and they wagered with one another for skins and knives.

The Englishmen spent another miserable night fighting fleas and mosquitoes in Massasoit's lodge. Although the Chief begged them to stay, they left at dawn the next morning. They had eaten only a little fish in two nights and a day and had had hardly any sleep. They were glad to be returning to Plymouth.

Of a Black Sheep and of a Strayed Lamb and of How Squanto Was Avenged

(August, 1621)

The Billingtons were one of the profanest families in Plymouth and had been shuffled into the "Mayflower" company at London. John Billington had refused to obey the orders of Captain Standish and had used some very bad language. As a punishment, he had been forced to spend a number of unpleasant hours on public display, with his neck and his heels tied together.

His two sons, John and Francis, were a wild

and vagrant pair. Francis had gone into the gun room of the "Mayflower" as she lay in Province-town Harbor, and had found a loaded musket, which he fired off. As there were powder barrels about and one was open, it was a miracle that the ship had not been blown out of the water. Later in Plymouth the boys had been strictly forbidden to go to the woods. Of course, Francis took the very first opportunity to explore the forest.

From the top of a high hill, where he had climbed a tree, he caught a glimpse of shining waters in the west. When he returned, he reported he had seen the western ocean. He and one of the sailors went inland for three miles and found the "ocean" to be two large fresh water lakes, out of which flowed the town brook. The lakes were full of fish and wild fowl. Folks said that Francis had made a valu-able discovery. The lakes were called "Billington's Sea."

Again the Billingtons stirred up Plymouth. John Junior had disappeared in the forest. It was ru-mored that he had been stolen by Indians. At first some people said that they felt sorry for the In-dians, but after five days, the village was very alarmed. A lost child was everybody's business and a search party was organized. Ten of the stoutest men went down the Cape in the shallop to search among the Indians. After a heavy storm, they put in for the night at Cummaguid Harbor (Barnstable Harbor).

Next morning the boat was left aground at low tide. Shoreward the searchers could see a party of Indians hunting for lobster. From them they learned, through Squanto, that John Junior was safe among the Indians at Nauset (Eastham.) The savages invited them ashore to share their lobster breakfast, then took them to their chief sachem whose name was Ivanough. He was the handsomest and most courteous Indian they had ever met.

As the Indians crowded around them, a squaw pushed forward to see the white men. She was so withered and wrinkled that they took her to be at least a hundred years old. She tottered forward and peered closely in their faces. Suddenly she burst into a loud wailing and began weeping bitterly.

After the hubbub had quieted somewhat, Squanto explained that the old squaw had once had three sons. They had gone aboard Hunt's trading vessel and had been carried off and sold in Spain, even as Squanto himself had been. Ever since, the mother had grieved, for she knew she would never see them again.

Captain Standish said, "Hunt is a bad man of whom the English are ashamed. We would not do such a thing for all the furs in the country." He tried to comfort the poor woman with some trinkets, which seemed to please her.

There was now hope that they would soon find young Billington alive among the Indians. It was again low tide when they reached Nauset. Darkness prevented them from entering the harbor, so Squanto and Ivanough were sent with a message to Aspinet, Sachem of Nausets, saying that the English had come to seek the lost boy.

Soon a band of the Nauset Indians came down to the shore and waded out to the grounded shallop. They urged the English to bring the boat ashore.

Captain Standish suddenly realized that these were the same Indians who had attacked them at the place of the First Encounter.

"Stand ready to fire," he ordered. Then, turning to Squanto, the Captain went on: "Squanto, tell them that only the Indians whose corn we have taken may come aboard."

Squanto explained to the two tall warriors who came aboard that the English wished to pay them for their corn. They would bring them the corn or the Indians could come to Patuxet (Plymouth) for it. The braves said they would like to come to Patuxet.

More Indians surrounded the shallop. Aspinet with fifty unarmed warriors had now joined them and behind him were fifty more waiting with their arrows on their bow strings. At this moment John Billington Junior arrived on the scene, perched triumphantly on the shoulders of a huge Indian. He was decked in feathers and necklaces of wampum and was having a wonderful time.

The boy was restored to his father. The Indian who had taken charge of him while he was a captive among them was given a knife. A few trinkets to Aspinet restored peace.

Sitting about the camp fire, the boy told of his adventures among the savages. He had had a good time with the Indian children and was well treated. He would be the hero of the hour in Plymouth when they returned. No wonder he was so pleased with himself!

Squanto returned to camp from the Nausets with alarming news. He had heard that the terrible Narragansetts were on the war path. Massasoit had been captured and some of his people killed. Plymouth was in danger, with only twenty-two men to defend her. Standish decided to return to the threatened settlement at once, for it was a forty-eight mile journey by sea. The wind was contrary but they started back without further delay. After a rough voyage they came to Plymouth at last and found all things well.

An Indian named Hobomok came running in from the woods with more alarming news. He and Squanto had gone in search of their Chief, Massasoit. They learned that he had been betrayed by one of his sachems, named Corbitant. This Indian was stirring up Massasoit's own people in revolt against him, and was speaking against the English.

Corbitant had taken Hobomok and Squanto prisoner, but Hobomok had managed to escape. The last he had seen of Squanto, he was being threatened by Corbitant with his knife. Corbitant had said that if Squanto were dead the English would lose their tongue. Hobomok was sure that by this time Squanto had been killed.

Captain Standish determined this insolence must be punished at once. If Squanto were dead, he must be avenged. At the head of his army of ten musketeers, Standish started out for Corbitant's village.

All day Standish and his men marched in the rain. At nightfall, Hobomok said they were approaching the Indian village. They halted for supper, left their heavy knapsacks behind, and advanced stealthily through the darkness.

Pressing on, they surrounded the village. Standish burst into Corbitant's lodge with his drawn sword, shouting, "Let no one move till we have taken Corbitant."

Several Indians who attempted escape were wounded in the scuffle. The soldiers fired their muskets. The whole town was in an uproar. The Indian women surrounded Hobomok and hung on his neck, seeking protection and calling him "towam," or friend. Seeing that the women were being spared, the Indian boys began crying out that they were girls.

Captain Standish was told that Squanto was still

alive. He ordered the campfires to be lighted and the lodges searched. Hobomok climbed atop a lodge and began calling for Squanto. He suddenly appeared in the circle of firelight. All the Indians then were disarmed.

In the morning it was found that Corbitant and his warriors were not there. The Indians were told that the English intended to destroy only Corbitant and would punish any who should attack Squanto or Massasoit.

The party then marched home with Squanto. Several friendly Indians followed with the baggage. Three wounded Indians were brought back with them for treatment.

"So that, by God's good providence, we safely returned home, the morrow night after we set forth."

It had been a wild night of shouting and drawn swords and the gleam of armor against the darkness of the forest. Fortunately no one had been seriously hurt. Although Corbitant had not been captured or punished, the power of the fiery little Captain and his army had struck terror into the hearts of the Indians.

Of the Arrival of the Ship "Fortune"

(November, 1621)

It was almost a year to a day from the time that the "Mayflower" had anchored in Cape Cod Bay. Seven houses stood on the hillside overlooking Plymouth Harbor and more were being built. The common storehouse was full of corn. The Pilgrims had fought starvation and won. No Indian attacks had been made on them from the threatening forests. By God's grace the savages were their friends.

For all this there was a price. Half of their company lay in unmarked graves. Each day they must labor, and watch by night against hunger and danger. Each day for a year, their tired eyes had watched the naked horizon and never a sail had come to bring them the promised supplies. Had they been utterly forgotten? Was there still an England?

Suddenly a cannon shot signaled the workers in from the woods and clearings. A sail on the horizon! Soon an English ship had anchored in the harbor. All Plymouth was at the water's edge to greet the men who stepped from the longboat. Their friend, Mr. Cushman, had come in the ship "Fortune," bringing thirty-five lusty young men. Some were members of the Leyden Church; all were good workers for the fields, and soldiers for defense. They were given welcome and then eager attention as they told news of home and friends.

Mr. Cushman delivered his letters to the Governor. It appeared that the "Fortune" had brought no supplies, not so much as a barrel of flour. The letter from the Merchant Adventurers was full of reproaches. The "Mayflower" had been sent back empty to England. The company would lose money.

"I know your weakness was the cause of it, and I believe more weakness of judgemente, than weakness of hands," said the letter. The "Fortune" must bring back a profitable cargo or the Adventurers might not invest further in Plymouth Plantation. A new contract was enclosed for the signatures of the colonists. In it they practically bound themselves to slavery to the Adventurers for seven years. Reluctantly they signed it.

In two weeks the "Fortune" sailed for England with a cargo of clapboard and two hogshead of beaver skins. This fur was unknown in England and had been first brought to Plymouth by Squanto.

As the "Fortune's" sail faded on the horizon, the colonists turned back to their labor. It seemed that the "Fortune" was a name that mocked their hopes of supply and comfort from England.

Of the Strange Message from Canonicus and Their Bold Reply

An Indian runner had brought the strange token and departed as silently as he had come. The snake skin with its black and brown patterns lay on the table like an evil thing. The light glistened on its shining scales and six arrows protruded from its gaping mouth. The thing had some meaning that boded no good. It had been sent to the Pilgrims by Canonicus, Chief of the Narragansetts.

At once Bradford sent for Squanto, Winslow, Brewster, Allerton, and Standish. Squanto told them that the snake skin meant that Canonicus planned war upon them. It was a message of defiance. The Elders debated whether to ask for peace or answer in kind.

Brewster contended they should send a message saying, "We would wish to have peace but if you want war, we are ready."

"Perhaps he will better understand this," said Bradford, snatching the arrows from the rattlesnake skin and filling it with powder and shot.

When the rattlesnake skin was returned to Canonicus he refused to accept or even touch it. He ordered it out of his sight, out of the village, out of his domain.

"It is the terrible medicine with which the English destroy our people and take from us the lands of our fathers," cried the terrified chieftain.

The snake skin was refused by one awed chieftain after another until it was finally returned to Plymouth.

(Thanksgiving, 1621)

In the spring rain and summer sun, the green stalks of the Indian corn grew tall. The firm ears became full and heavy, two and three on each stalk. The corn silk turned brown on the end of each ear and every tall stalk waved its feathery tassels like an Indian chief. Under Squanto's guidance the Pilgrims hoed and tended the corn hills through the hot summer days. Health and strength came back to the invalids and no one was sick.

The bay teemed with shad, cod, mackerel, and herring. Squanto showed the Pilgrims how to take lobsters and eels. He led them to where oyster and clam beds were most abundant. When the summer was done, the hard golden ears of corn were reaped and stored.

Now there was time to hunt in the forest. Flocks of fat wild turkeys trooped in the underbrush, and along the streams and marshes huge flocks of geese and ducks prepared for their southward flight. The black bear ambled under the oak trees seeking acorns, and the deer grazed on the southern slopes among the birch and pine trees.

In a single day the hunters killed enough turkeys to last for a week. Gratefully they gathered on Sabbath days and sang praise to God for his goodness and mercy to the children of men.

Now the forests were turning to autumn splendor of red and gold. It was a time for a celebration, for a feast of rejoicing, for a day of Thanksgiving.

The twelve women of New Plymouth began great preparations. From the kitchens came the savory smell of roasting geese and turkey. An abundance of corn bread and hasty pudding was being prepared. Stewed eels, boiled lobsters, and juicy clam stews simmered over the fires.

Before the feast, Squanto was sent with an invitation to Massasoit and his chiefs. On the appointed day, the Chief appeared with ninety tall warriors. For a moment there was consternation among the cooks. They were not prepared to feed ninety extra guests, but Massasoit took care of the difficulty by sending his hunters into the forest. They returned with five deer. The feast now

became a barbecue with juicy cuts of roast venison for all.

There were shooting contests with bows and guns. The Plymouth Musketeers under their Captain, Miles Standish, put on a drill with drum and trumpet. In return the Indians performed their tribal dances and chants for the amazed English. Everyone relaxed. There was laughter and clowning. The Indians were in no hurry to go home as long as the food held out, and the holiday-making carried on for three days. Squanto and Samoset translated long speeches of friendship and good will. White men and red would keep the peace as long as the sun shone and the grass grew.

There would be lean times and hard work aplenty in the days ahead, but it was a goodly land. Though the English still were strangers in it, this was for them the Promised Land.

After the Thanksgiving feast, Plymouth settled down to its second winter. Daily Governor Bradford parceled out to each one a ration of corn from the common store. Because there were thirty-five newcomers to feed, he had to cut the corn rations to half of what had been planned at harvest time. When snow came, the hunters found no game in the bare woods. Each day the Governor sent the axemen to the forest to cut wood for the fires that must be kept burning in Plymouth against the bitter cold.

Christmas Day was no exception. That morning the newcomers came to the Governor and explained it was against their conscience to work on Christmas Day. "Very well, until you learn better," said the Governor as he marched off with the workers to the woods.

When the workers came home at noon, they found some of the newcomers playing games in the street, "some pitching ye bar and some at stoole-ball and suchlike sports." The Governor gathered up the gaming implements and drily announced that it was against *his* conscience for some to play while others worked. Through the bleak winter months, the men soon learned that hard work was not a virtue in Plymouth. It was a necessity.

In March a meeting was called to plan the second spring planting. The Governor divided up their common land and gave to each his lot, together with his share of the seed corn. This had been carefully saved from the common supply. It was now clear that they would not have enough food to last until the harvest. For weeks to come they would again have to fight off starvation as best they could while they waited for the crops to ripen.

Although Bradford's bold answer to Canonicus discouraged the Narragansetts from making war, there was still danger. Standish pointed out that the little group of houses on the hill slope was unprotected. His plan was to build a log palisade to enclose the Mount, as well as the town, down to the water's edge. Everybody agreed to the plan. Axemen felled the straight pine trunks, and others worked on the six-foot-deep trench encircling the town.

Within a month a stout log palisade twelve feet high enclosed the town. At the corners were projecting bastions that commanded the sides. At sunset the gates were closed and a guard kept watch during the night.

Captain Standish was very proud of the new fortification. He proceeded to organize his fighting men into four companies with a leader for each. Each soldier was assigned his post for defense, in case of an attack or fire. From now on the settlers slept more peacefully in their beds at night.

Of a Strange Plot

(Spring, 1622)

Miles Standish was not a captain to sit idly in the shelter of the new palisade. He decided they should let the Indians know that the English would not remain shut up in the town fearfully awaiting an attack. The Captain would go forth boldly among them, for Plymouth was badly in need of provisions and the Indians of Massachusetts were known to have much corn. The shallop was fitted out for this trip with trading goods, guns and gunpowder.

The Captain and his ten musketeers, together with Squanto and Hobomok, sailed out of the harbor for Massachusetts Bay. As they rounded the point called Gernet's Nose, the wind died down. Standish threw out the anchor while the men got out their oars.

Suddenly a distant cannon shot sounded across the water. Then another and then a third. It was a signal from Plymouth telling them to come back. They loaded their muskets and rowed with all speed.

At Plymouth they found every man and boy standing at his post prepared for an Indian attack. Squanto's brother had come running into the town, his face covered with blood, to warn them that the Narragansetts, together with Corbitant and Massasoit, were on the way to attack the town. The Indians, he said, were close behind him.

All night they stood watch. No Indians appeared. The messenger who brought the news had disappeared. It was a false alarm.

Not long after, Hobomok came secretly to Standish, saying he knew that his chief, Massasoit, would not make war on the English. It was a plot by Squanto to turn the English against Massasoit.

When Standish said he could not believe this of their faithful friend, Squanto, Hobomok revealed that Squanto, for a long time, had been terrifying the Indians. It had been his boast that he had great power to influence the English to destroy the tribes. He had told them that the English kept the dreadful plague hidden in the ground. Only he could prevent the white men from loosing it upon the Indians. Squanto was blackmailing the Indians and influencing them against Massasoit.

To prove this story, Hobomok said he would send his wife secretly to Massasoit's village to discover whether he was plotting against the English. She came back with word from Massasoit that he alway had and always would keep the peace treaty with his friends, the English. Squanto was a bad man and should die, Massasoit declared.

At this news, Standish angrily told Squanto that he deserved death. But he realized the Indian was too valuable to the English as an interpreter to be killed.

The expedition now set off again for Massachusetts and in a short time came back with a good supply of corn. On his return Standish found Massasoit in Plymouth, angrily demanding that

Squanto be killed for his treachery. In fact Massasoit wanted to murder the traitor on the spot
with his own axe. Bradford refused to surrender
Squanto, saying that he was "the tongue of the
English." Without him they would not be able
to talk with the Indians. Massasoit left in a rage.

A few days later messengers came from the
Chief with Massasoit's knife. With it the English
should kill Squanto and send his severed head and
hands to Massasoit. Squanto stood silently by
awaiting his fate. The Indians claimed that he was
Massasoit's subject and according to the peace
treaty must be turned over to them.

At this moment a cannon shot announced a sail
on the horizon. The lookout reported that it appeared to be a pirate ship. The Governor ordered
everyone on the alert. Bradford told the Indians
that they must await his decision about Squanto.
Waiting was not an Indian virtue and the savages
left in a fury.

Of How They Built a Strong Fort for Their Defense

The sail was not a French pirate ship, but a shallop with an English crew from one of Mr. Weston's fishing vessels, "The Sparrow." It had come to deliver seven passengers from Leyden. The visitors brought no supplies other than enough for the return of the shallop's crew.

These new arrivals added seven more mouths for

Plymouth to feed, besides the thirty-five men from the "Fortune." Their provisions were nearly exhausted.

In desperation, Bradford decided to send to the fishing fleet for provisions. He appointed Winslow to this difficult business. He had been a wise ambassador on all occasions.

Winslow now took the long trip up the east coast in the shallop and found the "Sparrow" and the fishing fleet. When he told them of Plymouth's desperate need, the fishermen gave him what they could spare. Winslow returned with enough food to provide a lean diet till harvest time.

In this desperate situation, Standish, Bradford, and Elder Brewster sat in the meeting house considering future plans. "The Indians, knowing of our poor condition, grow daily more insolent, and Massasoit hath taken much offense and cometh no more unto us as formerly," said the Governor gloomily. Then he added, "Hunger and weakness doth greatly discourage our people."

"And the sin of idleness will do worse," said Captain Standish, rising and pacing the floor.

Brewster opened the great brass-studded Bible on the table before him.

"Lift up the hands that hang down, and strengthen ye the feeble knees," he read. "Thus sayeth the Prophet Isaiah."

"Methinks this is the Lord's counsel to us to arise and build a fort on top of the Mount, and there place our cannon. It will greatly set back our enemies," mused the Captain, looking out the window toward the Mount.

"Such a fort could serve as a meeting house and would greatly encourage our people in their worship of God," replied Elder Brewster vigorously.

At the town meeting every man's vote was cast in favor of building the fort. Soon the hills echoed with the clamor of axe and saw and hammer. Work took men's minds off the gnawing emptiness under their belts. They talked gayly, or grimly, and jested as they worked. It gave them a lift of heart to see the wooden walls rise higher day by day.

May came, and with it planting time. Shifts of workers left the fort and went to the fields to set corn. On the flat roof of the fort were planted four cannon. Within were a goodly meeting hall, a gun room for muskets and ammunition and a guardhouse where lawbreakers were to be kept.

"Now the fort is finished, we shall keep a guard there," said Mr. Winslow to the Captain as they stood on the roof of the new building and looked out over their fields green with new corn. "It will utterly discourage the savages from rising against us."

Concerning the Coming of the "Charity" and the "Swan" and of the Great Sickness That Came Upon Massasoit and of How Master Winslow Did Marvelously Recover Him

One day toward the end of June, two ships sailed into Plymouth Harbor. They were the "Charity" and the "Swan," sent by Mr. Weston in England to begin a plantation at Massachusetts Bay. The sixty newcomers asked to stay at Plymouth until their surveyors could find a good place to settle somewhere in Massachusetts.

The long-suffering colonists of Plymouth took these visitors into their homes and shared with them their lean rations in Christian charity. The Weston men proved themselves a graceless crew. Some helped to weed and tend the corn fields by day. Others by night stole and ate the unripe ears of corn.

At last this band of ruffians departed in the "Swan" for their new colony on the Bay, and the "Charity" returned to England. Before leaving for Massachusetts, the newcomers left their sick in the care of surgeon Samuel Fuller at his own charge. As they recovered the doctor sent them to Massachusetts.

Shortly after, the Bay Indians came to Bradford with bitter complaints that the newcomers were robbing the Indian corn fields. The Governor could do no more than advise the new settlers to deal honestly with the Indians. Before the coming of Weston's men, the Plymouth settlers had planned to start a trading post on the Bay.

By August, the provisions at Plymouth were exhausted. Two more ships arrived—the "Discovery," Thomas Jones, Master, and the "Sparrow," a smaller ship belonging to Weston. The "Sparrow" carried a cargo of fish.

Captain Jones of the "Discovery" had plenty of supplies which he was willing to sell, at top prices, though he demanded in exchange beaver skins at below their current market value.

These unlooked-for provisions were enough to keep them till harvest time.

"Had not the Almighty in his all-ordering Providence, directed him to us; it would have gone worse with us than ever it had been, or after was."

The unruly Weston colony at Wessagussett (Weymouth) on the Bay soon used all their provisions. Winter was at hand. They sent to Plymouth, proposing that the two plantations join in trading along the coast with the Indians for corn. The Weston men would furnish their ship "Swan" for this purpose and the proceeds would be divided between them.

The Plymouth colony agreed, but Standish, their usual leader, was sick with fever and so Governor Bradford led the expedition. Squanto, too, went along promising to guide the "Swan" around the Cape and through the shoals of Pollack's Rip. Not long after they left the harbor, fierce winter storms beat upon them, and forced them to turn back. However, they traded with the Cape Indians and collected some twenty-eight hogshead of corn.

During this voyage, Squanto was taken ill with an Indian fever. Within a few days he died, asking the Governor to pray for him, that he might go to the Englishmen's God in heaven.

The corn was divided and the Weston colonists returned to Wessagussett. Captain Standish had now recovered and went along the Cape in the shallop, trading for corn in the bitter January weather. Through the long winter, he came and went, trading and treating with the thieving, treacherous Indians. Once he barely escaped an Indian plot on his life by "a notable insulting villain," Witawamat, whose hands were stained with the blood of many a castaway English and Frenchman. The fearless Captain and his men in the weather-beaten shallop came back with corn enough to keep alive the families in the Plymouth cabins. The flame of hope and faith was kept aglow through the lean winter days and nights.

One day, an Indian came with news that Massasoit was sick unto death. The Plymouth folk had not heard of the Chief since the quarrel over Squanto, but this was not the time to harbor ill will. After all, the great Chief had been and still was their faithful ally. Bradford appointed Winslow to visit the sick sachem. With him went Master John Hamden, a visiting gentleman from London who wanted to see the country. Hobomok was their guide.

On the way, they heard that the Chief was dead. When they reached Massasoit's village, they found that the sachem was still alive. From his lodge came the chanting of the medicine men. Enough din to make a well man sick, thought Winslow. The lodge was crowded with sorrowing friends who believed their Chief as good as dead. Six squaws sat around the sick man, chafing his arms and legs.

Winslow saw at once that Massasoit was indeed at the point of death. He had lost his sight and his jaws were set. As the Englishman leaned over him, the dying man reached out a feeble hand and groaned, "Keen Winsnow (Is this you, Winslow?)" for the Indians could not say "L." "Oh, Winsnow, I shall never see you again."

Winslow explained, through Hobomok, that the Governor had sent him to say how sorry he was to hear of his friend's sickness. He had sent medicine and such things as he thought most likely to do him good. If Massasoit would take it, Winslow would give him the medicine at once.

Winslow had to force the concoction between the Indian's clenched teeth with his knife. The sick man swallowed for the first time in two days. The Englishman then washed his mouth and scraped his furred and swollen tongue. In a few moments the sick man asked for a drink and the amateur doctor poured more medicine down his throat. Within half an hour Massasoit opened his eyes.

Winslow leaned close to his face and smiled. "Massasoit will live," he said. "Soon he will be restored to health and strength."

In a few moments Massasoit was asleep for the first time in days. Winslow sent off a note to surgeon Samuel Fuller asking for more physic and a couple of chickens with seasoning for a broth.

Among the Indians the news spread that the sachem had been restored to health. A miracle had been brought about by the white man's medicine.

When the Chief awoke he was hungry. He asked

Winslow to make him some soup of wild duck such as he had tasted at Plymouth.

At once Winslow set to work to prepare a thin soup of corn meal flavored with strawberry leaves and sassafras root. After eating this, the Chief was strong enough to sit up.

Massasoit's confidence in Winslow was now boundless. He insisted that the Englishman visit every sick Indian in the village and give him the same treatment. It was an unfamiliar task for Winslow, but he did the best he knew and went among the sick in the foul-smelling lodges. "With wonderment he blessed God for giving His blessing to such raw and ignorant means."

After Winslow had seen all the other sick and ailing Indians, Massasoit wanted more broth. Winslow took his gun and soon came back with a fat duck. Presently the savory soup was ready. Winslow told Hobomok to skim the fat from the top as it was entirely too rich for the weak stomach of the convalescent. But Massasoit would not permit it and quickly swallowed several helpings of the rich dish.

In an hour the sachem was again a very sick man. He was vomiting and, what was worse, bleeding severely from the nose. This, the Indians believed, was a sure sign of death. But presently the bleeding ceased and Massasoit slept as Winslow watched by his side. When he woke, Winslow bathed his face and urged his friend to take things slowly until he was stronger. He soon could sit up and receive visitors.

When the chickens were brought from Plymouth the Chief decided he would not eat them. Instead he would keep them and start a poultry farm.

Massasoit's Indian friends came from as far as a hundred miles to see the miracle. The Chief told them, "Now I see the English are my friends and love me; and whilst I live I will never forget this kindness they have showed me."

Of How Massasoit Disclosed a Most Villainous Plot and of the Bold Actions of Captain Standish

On the night before the Englishmen were to return to Plymouth, Massasoit gave Hobomok a secret message for Winslow. Hobomok confided it to him as they marched homeward through the woods. The Indians were planning to attack and destroy the two English colonies. The Massachusetts, the Narragansetts, the Cape Cod Indians and even those of the Isle of Capawack (Martha's Vineyard) were in league to wipe out Weston's colony because of their many crimes against the Indians. After this they would destroy Plymouth.

Massasoit had been pressed to join the others, but had not done so. He urged that Governor Bradford find and kill the conspirators at once. If they should wait until they were attacked, it would then be too late.

No one knew better than Winslow how weak were the two little towns on the ocean frontier. He and his party hurried on through the forest toward Plymouth. That evening they accepted an invitation from their old enemy Corbitant to spend the night at his lodge. It was a chance to get better acquainted with a powerful chief and perhaps pick up further news of what was afoot.

They spent a rare night in talk at Corbitant's lodge.

"How did two men alone dare come so far into the Indian's country?" asked Corbitant.

" 'Where was true love, there was no fear,' " parried Winslow, quoting his Bible.

"Then why, when we come to Patuxet, do you stand guard and point your guns at us?" the Indians asked:

"On land and sea the English thus salute those they wish to honor," said Winslow.

Corbitant shook his head and said he liked not such salutation.

"Why do you ask a blessing on your meals before you eat, and give thanks for the same?" the savage asked more seriously.

Winslow was now on firm ground of Puritan doctrine as he explained, "Whatsoever good things we had, we received them of God, as the Author and Giver thereof, and therefore craved His blessing on that we had, and were about to eat, that it might nourish and strengthen our bodies; and having eaten sufficient, being satisfied therewith, we again returned thanks to the same our God, for that our refreshing."

Corbitant said that this was good, and that the Indians believed almost all the same things; and that the same power we called God, they called "Kietitan."

This caused Mr. Winslow to change his views about Indian godlessness. He now went on with growing fervor to explain about "God's works of Creation and Preservation; of His laws and ordinances, especially of the Ten Commandments: all of which they hearkened unto with great attention; and liked well of." Perhaps they excepted the Seventh Commandment, which Corbitant thought held a man down too strictly to one wife. "About which, we reasoned a good time." Winslow always remembered that night as the most interesting he had ever spent among the Indians.

Hurrying on next day, they met Indians who said that Standish had gone to Massachusetts. On their arrival at Plymouth, they found Standish had returned, being providentially turned back by contrary winds.

At Plymouth, too, they learned that a messenger had brought a letter from Sanders, the overseer at the Bay colony. The people of the colony had eaten their seed corn. They had traded everything, even their shirts, to the Indians for corn. Now the Indians refused to sell them any more. Sanders proposed attacking the Indians and taking their corn by force. Would Plymouth join them in making war? It had always been the policy of Plymouth never to attack the Indians but to stand on the defense. They sent word to Sanders, urging him not to attack the Indians.

After he had heard this news, Winslow told

about the Indian conspiracy and Massasoit's advice to seize the conspirators and thus break up the plot. Immediately all Plymouth was called to a meeting to decide what must be done. Plainly it would be dangerous this time to wait for the Indians to attack. So Bradford, Allerton, and Standish were appointed to determine what action to take. Standish was instructed to go to the Bay with as many men as he chose and tell them of the plot. He was not to make trouble with the Indians, but seek out the conspirators and deal with them, especially their chief, that "bloody and bold villain" Witawamat, whose head he was expressly ordered to obtain.

Captain Standish picked eight of his best men. A greater number might excite the Indians' suspicion. The shallop was made ready with arms and provisions. Tomorrow she would set sail on her dangerous mission. Danger was the Captain's business and he was never happier than when he was facing it. At last he would come to grips with that notable villain Witawamat.

How Witawamat Lost His Head

The company in the shallop made a forty-mile run along the coast in a fair breeze. Sheltered in a deep bay, they found the "Swan" at anchor. When they came alongside and hailed her, there was no answer. Climbing aboard, they found no one on the ship—not even a dog. Perhaps they had come too late. Had the Indians massacred the colony?

They fired off a musket and then another. The shot echoed across the water. Presently they heard a shout. On the wooded shore they could see white men. It was the master of the "Swan" and her crew.

"But why have you abandoned the ship?" the amazed Captain Standish asked the "Swan's" master.

"Oh, we get along very well with the Indians, practically lived among them," the master replied. "We have no need of either guns or swords."

To this Captain Standish answered somewhat drily, "If there is no need, I am the gladder."

Standish was then told that Sanders had gone on a voyage to the fishing fleet, seeking provisions. In the meantime the Captain would find Sanders' lieutenants at the town near by.

To the shiftless crew at Wessagusset, Standish explained the Indian plot and offered to take back to Plymouth anyone who wanted to go. All the men were ordered in at once from the outlying woods and camps.

That day an Indian slunk into the post from the forest with his furs to trade. When he returned to his tribe, he reported that he had seen in the Captain's eyes that he was angry in his heart. This Englishman had discovered their secret.

Next day a tall savage, who said his name was Pecksuot, came into the town and talked with

Hobomok. "Tell the Captain we know but fear him not, neither will we shun him," said Pecksuot. "But let him begin when he dare; he shall not take us unaware."

The Captain was not accustomed to such talk from an Indian. More Indians came and there were more insulting speeches. The braves sat in the compound sharpening their knives in the Captain's very face. He choked down his rage and said nothing.

One morning as Standish sat cleaning his musket, the door of his cabin softly opened. There stood before him the powerful figure of Witawamat. Across his nose were painted three black stripes. His eyes glittered in his dark face and on his brutal mouth was a faint smile. He lifted the knife that hung from a cord about his neck. Pointing to the handle, on which was crudely cut the face of a woman, he said with an insolent sneer, "I have another at home with which I have killed many French and English. On it is a man's face. By and by these two shall marry."

Pecksuot, who had come in without knocking, began a speech in which he implied that the Captain was a cowardly runt who should be at work in the fields with the women. Standish understood enough Indian to get the full import of the insult and his anger strained like a hound on the leash, but he made no reply. As Witawamat left he pointed again to his knife and said, "By and by it shall see; by and by it shall eat but not speak."

"You shall soon have a lesson in talking knives," muttered the Captain to himself.

Next day four Indians came to the Captain's house. Witawamat brought with him his brother, a young Indian of about eighteen. The gigantic Pecksuot was accompanied by a savage nearly his size and of equally villainous expression. The Indians, as usual, were naked to the waist. From their necks hung sheathed knives. There were three soldiers in the room besides Standish and Hobomok. Each Englishman wore a steel corselet.

When the Indians were all in the room, Standish nodded his head slightly. At the signal Hobomok noiselessly closed and barred the door. Pecksuot began a bragging speech. In the middle of it Standish made a sudden leap and, snatching the Indian's knife from its sheath, buried it to the hilt in his breast. In an instant the room was a shambles of struggling men and stabbing knives.

Witawamat, bleeding from a dozen terrible

knife wounds, rolled on the floor, grappling with his attacker. With unbelievable toughness and strength the Indians kept up the unequal fight. Hobomok stood motionless against the wall, coolly watching the fierce action. Pecksuot in his death agony still grappled with the Captain.

Suddenly it was over. Three bodies lay on the floor in pools of blood. The youngest Indian had somehow escaped with a few cuts. "Take him out and hang him to the nearest tree at once," ordered Standish. He bent over the body of Witawamat and with the Indian's own knife severed the head.

Hobomok stepped forward and with his foot pushed the body, contemptuously saying, "Yesterday Witawamat say he big and strong. He say Captain little man. Today little Captain big enough to lay Witawamat on the ground."

The Weston men refused to return to Plymouth with Standish. They joined the fishing fleet and returned to England.

All Plymouth turned out to welcome the return of the shallop. Standish marched up the Fort Hill at the head of his little troop. In the crowded meeting house he drew from its bag the bloody head of Witawamat and held it on high. It was placed

on a pike on the wall of the fort, after the English custom, as an example to enemies.

This was a day of triumph and thanksgiving. Elder Brewster said that Captain Standish had been a David and a Gideon unto them and had greatly cast down their enemies.

The fate of the chief conspirator Witawamat spread terror through the forest and the Indian confederacy was broken up. Whole tribes left their fields and villages and fled in terror to the swamps where many died from disease and starvation.

In the abandoned compound of Weston's colony at Wessagusset, the grass and weeds grew, and the sumac and the goldenrod took possession. The Indians avoided the neighboring forest, where the spirits of Pecksuot and the headless Witawamat walked in the moonlight when the wind wailed and mourned in the naked treetops.

Of How Began Free Enterprise Because Some Wished Not to Work for the Community: and of the Sore Drought That Came Upon Them

(1623)

Spring had come. It was March and the frost had come out of the hard ground, leaving soft and wet mud. The last handfuls of corn were being given out in equal rations from the common store. Only the precious seed corn for planting was left. On it depended the settlers' survival from starvation. The time for their third planting was at hand. Each year the Governor divided the common land equally among the families. The soundest church members usually got the best lots.

Last year this had caused discontent and there had been grumbling. Some were workers and some were shirkers, but all received equal amounts of food from the common supply. This was taken up at the town meeting. It was decided that each family should keep the crop it raised on its allotted land. Each little farm would be a free enterprise. There would be no more common store. Each would work for himself.

The result was wonderful. Each family, even the women and the children, worked in the fields daily from dawn till dark. Every inch of each field was planted and tended. There never had been such a planting. They had no plows, horses, or oxen. With spades and mattocks they loosened the earth, planted two fish in each hill, and dropped in the hard kernels. At night they took turns watching to keep the wolves from digging up the fish. The lean and ragged colonists tended their greening fields

with a new pride and energy. The laziness and in-
difference of "communitie" had vanished like the
sea mist before the sun.

It would be weeks before their crops were ripe.
They had long ago ceased expecting a supply ship
from England. In summer the wild fowl were hard
to shoot. Each day now starvation stared them in
the face.

At their feet the great bay was teeming with cod,
herring, bass, a dozen kinds of fish. They had seen
grampus, whale and seal. Squanto had showed them
where there were shellfish and eels in abundance.
They were used to the roast beef of old England
and to the bread, cheese and butter of Holland, and
they hated fish. But now if they would not starve
they must take the harvest of the sea.

There was only one boat but they worked it in
relays. One crew took her out as soon as another
came in.

> *"Neither did they return until they had
> caught something, though it were five or six
> days before, for they knew there was nothing
> at home, and to go home empty would be a great
> discouragement to ye rest."*

When the shallop was out long or came back with a small catch, the men dug clams from the mud at low tide and caught lobsters, crabs and shellfish. Now and then the hunters brought in a deer or two from the woods. From day to day they lived on what the Lord provided and were thankful.

May passed with fair weather. Indeed, the weather was too good. Day after day, they watched the unclouded sky as the corn drooped and turned yellow for lack of rain. It had not rained for six weeks. Hopes of the abundant harvest from their well-tilled fields faded.

"UPON WHICH THEY SETT APARTE A SOLEMNE DAY OF HUMILIATION, TO SEEK YE LORD BY HUMBLE & FERVENTE PRAYER, IN THIS GREAT DISTRESE."

All day in the crowded meeting house on the hill they prayed, thanking God for His blessings. The service had continued over eight hours and the sun had shone all day in the brassy July sky.

"For all ye morning, and the greatest part of the day, it was clear weather & very hotte, and not a cloud or any signe of raine to be seen, yet toward evening it begane to be overcast, and

173

shortly after to raine with such sweete and gentle
showers, as gave them cause of rejoyceing &
blessing God. It came without either wind, or
thunder, or any violence, and by degreese in that
abundance, as that ye earth was thorowly wete
and soaked therwith. Which did so apparently
revive & quicken ye decayed corne & other
fruits, as was wonderful to see, and made ye In-
deans astonished to behold: and afterwards the
Lord sent them shuch seasonable showers, with
interchange of faire warm weather, as through
His blessing caused a fruitful & liberall harvest,
to their no small comforte & rejoyceing. For
which mercie (in time conveniente) they also
sett aparte a day of thanksgiving."

Of How Came the Good Ship "Anne" and the Pinnace "Ye Little James" with Many Goodly People and of How Each Gathered His Corne in Abundance

(August, 1623)

August came. The tasseled corn waved its green banners to the sun. The silk on the full ears was turning brown.

The boom of the signal gun turned all eyes seaward to where a fleck of a sail gleamed on the horizon. It was the supply ship "Anne". Ten days later her consort, the pinnace "Little James", came in. The two had been separated in heavy weather at sea. Together they brought sixty new colonists to Plymouth. Many were from the Leyden congregation. Among them were wives and children of men who had been waiting for them for three years.

Of the rest, Bradford wrote:

"Some of them being very useful persons, and became good members of ye body, and some were so bad, as they were faine to be at charge, to send them home againe ye next year."

The new arrivals were dismayed at the gaunt and ragged veterans of New Plymouth who welcomed them on the beach. Some were discouraged by the meager meal of fish and lobster without bread, and a cup of cold spring water, that was offered them.

The colonists had discovered in America that water was an attractive and healthy drink but in England most men drank only beer and looked on water as unhealthy and dangerous.

Sixty more new mouths to feed raised serious problems. Later at harvest time the Plymouth planters would have plenty. In the meantime, the newcomers were afraid that the planters would soon eat up the provisions they had brought. So it was agreed, and sanctioned before Governor Bradford, that the planters should keep all of their crops if they did not accept any of the newcomers' supply. The newcomers could keep the provisions they had brought, if they did not claim any of the planters' corn when the harvest was ripe.

All law-abiding newcomers not of the Plymouth company were welcomed to the colony, but they must donate an annual bushel of corn to the general store kept for emergency, and serve in the common defense. They would not have trading privileges with the Indians, because this trade the Pilgrims kept strictly for themselves.

That year each family gathered the full ears and brought in great heaping baskets to fill their bins with golden plenty. Under the new system, those who had abundance could sell or barter with those who would buy.

"Some of ye abler sorte and more industrious had to spare, and sell to others, so as any generall wante or famine hath not been amongst them since to this day."

The Sailing of the "Anne" and of the Great Fire That Perilously Threatened the Community Provision but Was Notably Prevented and Assuaged

The "Anne" was taking on her cargo of clapboard and all the beaver and other skins the colony had. She was taking back a few passengers who had come over to visit the country and others who, being discontented, did not want to remain.

The crews of the "Anne" and the "Little James" were ashore. They had assembled about a keg of rum in a house adjoining the general storehouse, and were making a night of it with songs and drunken gaiety around the fireplace, where flames blazed against the cold. The fire roared up the chimney and a stiff wind sent the sparks swirling in the darkness. A spark started a fire in the thatched roof, and it soon blazed up in the wind.

The dreaded cry "Fire" rang through the town.

"SAVE THE STORE HOUSE OR WE BE OVERTHROWN," CRIED THE CAPTAIN.

Men rushed into the blazing building with wet blankets and beat the flames back from the storehouse. But the wind had carried the flaming sparks to the roofs of neighboring houses. Two, three, four houses were ablaze. The wind whipped the flames into a devouring furnace. In the lurid light, men and women rushed to and fro, etched against the blackness of the night.

Some urged Standish to throw the goods out of the storehouse before the fire reached it. But as the Captain scanned the evil faces of the drunken seamen, he saw that they were hungry for loot and at once he ordered his soldiers to guard the storehouse and allow no one to enter.

Furiously the men of Plymouth beat at the

flames and the women brought water and wet blankets. Some one yelled mockingly, "Look out, take a good look around and you will see some who are not your friends." The rumor spread that the fire was the result of a wicked plot to rob the storehouse.

The flames reduced everything around the storehouse to smoldering embers, but the building itself was saved. The blackened framework of the adjoining houses stood stark against the dying fires. In the ruins of the house where the fire had started, a smoldering firebrand was found against the wall where it had been thrust in among dried leaves. It could not possibly have come there by accident. This discovery was certain evidence of the hand of villainy. Whatever had been the evil intent, Plymouth had again been saved from ruin.

The burned houses were those assigned to newcomers who were not of the company. As these people were now homeless, most of them took passage on the "Anne" for England. For which there was small regret either among those who left or those who stayed.

As the "Anne" with her villainous crew dropped below the horizon, Governor Bradford turned back toward the town with a sigh of relief. By the grace of God, Plymouth had frustrated Indians, traitors, rogues, drought, fire and starvation. The settlers had begun a great work, and none would leave it until it was finished or the doing was passed on to those who would follow.

Good News from New England
(September, 1623)

Bradford had grown weary of the complaining and accusing letters from the Merchant Adventurers in England; weary of waiting for supply ships that brought more hungry mouths to feed, but never a barrel of flour.

He must send someone to London to tell the truth about Plymouth. It must be someone who could wheedle out of those scheming tradesmen the tools and supplies to keep the Plymouth folk alive in a desolate land.

Winslow could tell the story, for he had lived every grim day of it. This man who had dealt with savages in the forests of new England could surely deal with the schemers of old England.

More important, Winslow had written a day-by-day story of New Plymouth from the beginning. This he would have printed in London for all England to read. Being something of a merchant himself and a good advertiser, Winslow shrewdly called the pamphlet "Good News from New England". It was a stirring tale manfully told and ended with these stout words:

"*If ever any people in these later Ages, were upheld by the Providence of God, after a more special manner than others: then we: and therefore are the more bound to celebrate the memory of His goodness, with everlasting thankfulness.*

"*For in these fornamed straits, such was our state, as, in the morning, we had often our food to seek for the day: and yet performed the duties of our Callings. I mean the other daily labors, to provide for aftertime. And though, at some times, in some season, at noon, I have seen men stagger, by reason of faintness for want of food: and yet ere night by the good Providence and blessing of God, we have enjoyed such plenty, as though the windows of heaven had been opened unto us.*

"*How few, weak and raw were we at our first*

beginning, and there settling: and in the midst of barbarous enemies! Yet God wrought our peace for us.

"How often have we been at the pit's brim, and in danger to be swallowed up: yea, not knowing until afterward that we were in peril? And yet God preserved us. Yea, and from how many that we yet know not of: He that knoweth all things best can tell.

"So that when I seriously consider of things, I cannot but think that God hath a purpose to give that land, as an inheritance, to our nation."

He knew that this would sound well in Puritan ears, and so with this first American scripture in his pocket he went aboard the "Swan."

From the ship's deck he watched New Plymouth recede slowly into the blue haze of the New England coast. The coast itself faded and vanished presently as the west wind filled the sails of the "Swan" bound for England.

Twenty Years Later

(1648)

Bradford laid his goosequill pen on the cluttered desk. At last he had finished it—the story of Plymouth from the beginnings up to now. None knew it better than himself. This was the story of the forty years he had lived since he had joined the Separatists at Scrooby. Those who came after would want to know how it was in the beginning with those who came first.

He had set down the story briefly and plainly, not glossing over any matter, but bluntly stating truth. After Plymouth had prospered, mischievous men had come seeking to sow strife and discord for their own gain. But the Lord's faithful had stood together in unity and had undone their wicked designs. These schemers and rioters had been patiently reproved. Those who had been found guilty after a fair trial had been put out of the colony or sent back to England.

Bradford looked across the Bay, sparkling blue in the afternoon sun. His gaze traveled to the horizon; his thoughts went back through the long years

ELDER BREWSTER

to his youth, and to Austerfield and Scrooby, where it all began. He had not changed; only that he was surer now and saw Truth clearer.

Outside, in the garden, he could see children playing. They had been born in Plymouth, like their fathers and mothers before them. These boys and girls were the grandchildren of the First Comers. There were still living in this year 1648, by the grace of God, thirty of the Old Stock who had come in the "Mayflower."

The seed of Liberty had taken root in this New England earth. A tree had sprung up that would some day fill the whole world. Truth seekers, like the fowls of the air, would find shelter in its branches. Each year, thousands were coming in crowded ships. New England was dotted with growing towns as far as the Connecticut Valley. Even beyond, young men with axes and plows and Bibles were pushing into the westward forest, saying:

"IT IS NOT WITH US AS WITH OTHER MEN WHOM SMALL THINGS CAN DISCOURAGE, OR SMALL DISCONTENTMENTS CAUSE TO WISH THEMSELVES AT HOME AGAIN."